Kingdom I entrusted to  rt
and union with Divine L
"Holy Love is the h_t is
the interpretation of the Law and the means of all sanctification."
"The will of man must choose Holy Love. It is not open to debate, and stands undaunted in the face of discernment. Holy Love cannot be judged, for it is the judge."
"Holy Love is offered in every present moment and follows the soul into eternity." *(June 28, 1999)*

THE EFFECTS OF HOLY LOVE IN THE HEART

"I have come to you to speak about the effects of Holy Love in the heart."

- "Holy Love can transform the most mundane task into a powerful redemptive tool in the Hands of God."
- "Holy Love, when it is accepted in the heart, can transform darkness into the Light of Truth."
- "Holy Love can inspire victory over sin; therefore, Holy Love is the foundation of every conversion of heart."
- "Holy Love is the vehicle of surrender of free will to accept God's Divine Will."
- "It is Holy Love which helps the soul to recognize God's Grace in every cross."

"These are sound reasons for souls to accept these Messages and to support this Mission of Holy Love by living the Messages. To do so is to allow your heart to be transformed by Holy Love. To do so is to follow the pursuit of Holy Perfection." *(St. Francis de Sales – January 14, 2012)*

"Without Holy Love in the heart, good deeds, penance and reparation are hollow; for Holy Love is the foundation of holiness, righteousness and Truth. It is impossible for the soul to comply with the Divine Will of the Father apart from Holy Love, for God's Will is Holy Love."

"Holy Love leads the soul away from focus on self to focus on God and neighbor. This leads the heart into balance with the Divine Will. The soul gradually loses sight of how everything affects him – to focus on how everything affects God and neighbor. Such a soul is a jewel in God's Eyes and mounts swiftly up the Stairway to Holiness. This is the path to perfection." *(St. Francis de Sales – January 16, 2012)*

Comparison of Self-Love vs. Holy Love

Self-Love	Holy Love
Is motivated towards self-advantage in thought, word, and deed.	Is motivated in every thought, word, and action by love of God, and neighbor as self.
Sees only others' faults, not his own. Considers himself on the right path – perhaps even humble and virtuous.	Sees himself full of imperfections. Is always seeking to be perfected through love. Considers everyone more humble and holy than himself.
Holds a checklist in his heart of every wrong perpetrated against him.	Imitates Divine Mercy as best he can. Is compassionate and forgiving.
Is quick to anger and stands vigil over his own rights making certain they are not transgressed.	Is patient. Takes note of others' needs and concerns.
Hangs on to his own opinions refusing to surrender to another viewpoint.	Offers his own opinions but listens to others and lends them equal merit with his own.
Takes pride in his own achievements. May even take pride in his spiritual progress.	Realizes all things proceed from God; that without God he is capable of no good thing. All good comes from grace.
Sees himself and the world as the be-all/end-all. His only pleasure is thus achieved through the world.	Takes joy in storing up heavenly treasure, in growing closer to God and deeper in holiness. Knows the difference between earthly pleasures and spiritual joy.
Uses the goods of the world to satisfy self.	Uses the goods of the world to satisfy quest for holiness.
Objects to every cross. Sees trials as a curse. Resents others' good fortune.	Surrenders to the cross through love as Jesus did. Sees crosses as a grace to be used to convert others.
Prays only for himself and his own needs.	Prays for all in need.
Cannot accept God's Will. Becomes bitter over trials.	Accepts God's Will with a loving heart even when difficult.

(Given to Maureen Sweeney-Kyle by Blessed Mother on August 18, 1997)

A Pilgrim's Guide to
MARANATHA
SPRING & SHRINE

–Home of Holy Love Ministries–

Third Edition

WE WELCOME ALL PEOPLE OF ALL FAITHS.
PRAYER IS A UNIVERSAL LANGUAGE.
All who come in pilgrimage here are invited to join us
in prayer and the peace that Heaven offers at this site.

Published by:
Archangel Gabriel Enterprises Inc.

DECLARATION

This is an updated and expanded edition of the *Pilgrim's Guide to Maranatha Spring & Shrine* published in 2019. Unless otherwise indicated, all of the Messages contained in this edition were given by Heaven to the American Visionary, Maureen Sweeney-Kyle.

Current Canonical Explanation:

RESPONSE TO APPARITIONS AND VISIONARIES FOR ROMAN CATHOLICS

Since the abolition of Canon 1399 and 2318 of the former Code of Canon Law by Paul VI in AAS58 (1966) page 1186, publications about new apparitions, revelation, prophecies, miracles, etc., have been allowed to be distributed and read by the faithful without the express permission of the Church, providing that they contain nothing which contravenes faith and morals. This means, no imprimatur is necessary.

**The Discernment of Visionaries
and Apparitions Today**

by Albert J. Hebert, S.M., Page III

© 2012–2022 Archangel Gabriel Enterprises Inc.
North Ridgeville, OH 44039 All rights reserved
ISBN: 978-1-937800-77-2

Contents

About Holy Love (inside front cover)

Section 1. About the Apparitions

The Apparitions Begin 7

Apostolic Missions 9

The Image of Mary, Refuge of Holy Love 10

The Complete Image of the United Hearts 12

The Chambers of the United Hearts 14

The Messages of Holy and Divine Love 16

Maranatha Spring and Shrine 16

Ecumenical Lay Apostolates 17

Mission Statement 18

Section 2. Pilgrimage Information

What is a Pilgrimage? 19

Why Make a Pilgrimage to Maranatha? 19

Pilgrimage Preparation 23

Travel/Transportation 25

Lodging 28

Frequently Asked Questions 29

Glossary of Frequently Used Terms 34

Section 3. Journey of Holiness

Entrance to Maranatha Spring and Shrine 35

Making the Journey of Holiness 37

1. The Sorrowful Mother Shrine and Lake of Tears 38

2. Our Lady at the Arbor 42

3. Lake of the Holy Angels 43

4. Chapel of the Holy Angels 44

5. God the Father Shrine 45

6. St. Michael Shrine and Lake 46

7. Memorial to the Unborn 47

8. International Shrine of the White Madonna 48

FIELD OF THE UNITED HEARTS 50

9. Maranatha Spring 51

10. United Hearts Shrine 53
11. United Hearts Chaplet Meditations *(via foot path)* 54
12. St. Pio of Pietrelcina (Padre Pio) Shrine..........................57
13. Stations of the Cross 58
14. St. Joseph Shrine and Lake 63
Special Graces and Blessings Received While Making the
    Journey of Holiness 64

Section 4. Aquinas Center

St. Thomas Aquinas Learning Center *(illustrations)* 67
1. Our Lady's Blessing Point *(alcove)*..............................69
2. St. Thomas Aquinas *(alcove)*....................................71
3. Our Lady of Grace 71
4. Missionary Image of Our Lady of Guadalupe 72
5. Relic – A Strand of Blessed Mother's Hair 73
6. Our Lady of Fatima..73

Section 5. United Hearts Chapel

United Hearts Chapel *(illustrations)*................................75
1. St. Jude Thaddeus 76
2. Jesus Crucified 76
3. St. John Vianney 77
4. St. Thérèse of Lisieux..78
5. St. Joseph and the Child Jesus 79
6. Image of the United Hearts of the Most Holy Trinity and
    Immaculate Mary 80
7. Mary, Refuge of Holy Love 82
8. Sacred Heart of Jesus 82
9. St. Martin de Porres..84

Appendices

A. Our Lady gives the World the Rosary of the Unborn and the
    Chaplet of the Unborn to end Abortion 85
B. Family Consecration to the United Hearts.........................94
C. Concerning Photographs 96

General Ministry Information *(inside back cover)*

Section 1.
About the Apparitions

THE APPARITIONS BEGIN

Maureen Sweeney-Kyle was born on December 12, 1940, on the Feast of Our Lady of Guadalupe. She resides with her husband, Don Kyle, at the site of the miraculous Maranatha Spring and Shrine. Our Lady first appeared to Maureen in January 1985 at St. Brendan Catholic Church in North Olmsted, Ohio, dressed in light pink and a smoky-lavender color.

"I was at Adoration at a neighborhood Church and Our Lady was suddenly just standing to the side of the Monstrance – She never puts Her Back to Jesus in the Blessed Sacrament. She had a large beaded rosary in Her Hands and I thought, 'Am I the only one seeing Her?' People were getting up and leaving or coming in and not paying any attention. All of a sudden, the fifty Hail Mary beads turned into the shapes of the fifty states (of the United States). Then She left. I didn't know why She was there, but I thought, 'Maybe She wants me to pray for the country.'"
– **Interview with Maureen Sweeney-Kyle in July 2006**

"I appeared to you (Maureen) first with the Rosary of States. It was an appeal to pray for your country. Years later, the Rosary of States broke when I returned to you (on July 13, 1997) in the same vision. The states slipped off and landed in a smoldering pile at My Feet. This represented God's Justice."
– **Message from Our Lady given on March 24, 1998**

"Dear children, you are engaged in war – spiritual and physical war. Your weapon is this." She holds up the Rosary of States. Then it changes into the Rosary of the Unborn.*
– Message from Our Lady given on August 21, 2016

*(*Our Lady first appeared to Maureen with the Rosary of the Unborn on October 7, 1997. See Appendix A for details.)*

Spiritual Directors:
Over the years, Maureen has been guided by various spiritual directors who have been experts in Marian Theology. *"My Messenger has many spiritual advisors and a competent spiritual director who reads all the Messages ... all of My Messenger's advisors are anonymous. Wisdom dictates so."* **(Jesus – August 12, 2008)**

On the joyful occasion of the visit by the Visionary, Maureen Sweeney-Kyle, with Pope John Paul II in August of 1999. Maureen's husband, Don Kyle (bottom right), Archbishop Gabriel Ganaka of Nigeria* (top left), and Rev. Frank Kenney, Maureen's Spiritual Director from 1994–2004 (top center), accompanied her on the visit.

*Archbishop Gabriel Gonsum Ganaka (1937–1999) was from Jos, Nigeria, and was one of Maureen's spiritual advisors in 1998–1999. He passed away in November of 1999 and his cause for Sainthood was begun in March of 2007.

Section 1. About the Apparitions   9

APOSTOLIC MISSIONS

During the early years of the Apparitions, Blessed Mother appeared to Maureen on a nearly daily basis and gave her a series of missions to accomplish.

1986 – 1990
OUR LADY, PROTECTRESS OF THE FAITH
(Promotion of the Title and the Devotion)

1990 – 1993
PROJECT MERCY
(Nationwide Anti-Abortion Rosary Crusades)

1993 – Present
The combined Revelations of **MARY, REFUGE OF HOLY LOVE** and the **CHAMBERS OF THE UNITED HEARTS**. In 1993, Our Lady asked that this Mission be known as **Holy Love Ministries** and then requested that the Ministry procure property for a shrine in Lorain County, Ohio. This was accomplished in 1995. This 115-acre shrine is now known as **Maranatha Spring and Shrine**, the home of Holy Love Ministries, an Ecumenical Lay Apostolate to make known to the world the Chambers of the United Hearts through the **Messages of Holy and Divine Love**.

"My Mission in the world was ecumenical – for all people and all nations – just as this Mission here today is ecumenical. It was never my intent that this Ministry be controlled by one group or recognized religion. Mankind must never try to control the movement of the Holy Spirit. He will not succeed in such an effort. The term 'ecumenical' removes this Mission from the scrutiny of control of one institution – which is good – and opens the benefits of all the graces to one and all. Therefore, do not feel if you do not belong to a certain faith you are not welcome here. All are welcome. All are invited to come and see."

(Jesus – April 6, 2015)

"This Mission is a sign in the world of trustful surrender to the inspiration of the Holy Spirit. It has been a venue for Me, My Son and the Holy Mother to speak to the heart of the world. We speak to direct and to protect mankind. The Trinity is alive and well here."

(God the Father – May 27, 2018)

THE IMAGE OF MARY, REFUGE OF HOLY LOVE

On **March 4, 1997,** Blessed Mother took Maureen's hand and assisted her in drawing the Image of Mary, Refuge of Holy Love, in order to depict how She looks to the Visionary, and to grant to the world a new source of grace.

Image of Mary, Refuge of Holy Love

Section 1. About the Apparitions 11

Promises Attendant to the Image of Mary, Refuge of Holy Love
(As given by Blessed Mother)

1. Many and particular graces will come through this Image. *(March 6, 1997)*

2. Satan flees before this Image. It leaves Satan in terror. *(April 6, 1997; June 1, 1997)*

3. It is a fortress against evil, against much that will occur in the world, and should stand guard over every heart and home. *(April 11, 1998; April 28, 1998)*

4. Each home should accept this Image as protection and shelter. Those that do so shall not have anything to fear in these tribulations which are at hand. *(April 9, 1998)*

5. It is the invocation *'Mary, Refuge of Holy Love, pray for us'* that is your protection and your defense. Dear children, rely on the Image of My Heart that reminds you of this certain Refuge. *(May 7, 1998)*

6. It carries with it very many special graces which the world needs today. *(January 19, 2010)*

7. It carries with it a call to conversion of heart – a call to renounce the false gods of self-love and to live in Holy Love. *(December 12, 2006)*

8. It brings with it spiritual healing and peace. *(May 15, 1997)*

9. Those who venerate this Image, either in picture or three-dimensional form, will be drawn into deeper personal holiness. Their thoughts, words and deeds will be clarified in Holy Love. *(January 19, 2010)*

"Promulgate the Image you have before you. In this Image is the culmination of all My Apparitions during this century. It is the Refuge of the Immaculate Heart spoken of at Fatima. It is the promise of an era to come spoken of at Garabandal. I speak of the crown over My Heart, which foretells the victory of the United Hearts and the triumph of the Church over evil. The cross on My

Hand represents a dogma which is coming – Co-Redemptrix. I am pointing to My Heart, calling humanity into this safe Refuge. This Refuge is Holy Love." **(Blessed Mother – July 30, 1997)**

THE COMPLETE IMAGE OF THE UNITED HEARTS OF THE HOLY TRINITY AND IMMACULATE MARY

As I (Maureen) was praying in my prayer room, a large Flame appeared. Then I heard a voice that said: *"All praise be the Blessed Trinity. I am God the Father. You see My Heart before you as a massive Flame. It is the Flame of My Eternal, Divine Will which burns before you. It is this Flame that is the embodiment of Perfect Love and My Divine Will. My Heart is a Flame which engulfs the United Hearts of Jesus and Mary – of Holy and Divine Love – melting Them into Divine Union with My Will, never to be separated."*

"So you see, I present to you a new Image – the Complete Image of Love – the Union of Holy and Divine Love completely immersed in the Flame of My Fatherly Heart, which is the Divine Will. Remembering that My Will is made up of Divine Love and Divine Mercy, you must see My Heart as the Will of Mercy and Love. It is the perfection I invite all people and all nations to step into, beginning with the Heart of Mary. It is Eternally My Will in you." **(THE ETERNAL FATHER – January 18, 2007)**

"The Light which surrounds the Image of the United Hearts is the Light of the Holy Spirit, which inspires the soul to enter into a relationship with Holy and Divine Love. It is the Holy Spirit that leads the soul through the process of purification and challenges the heart to go deeper and ever deeper into Divine Love." **(St. Thomas Aquinas – February 17, 2007)**

"My brothers and sisters, accept the Image of Our United Hearts as the visual of My Father's Divine Will. It is He who sent Me to tell you this and to give you this Image. The Sacred Chambers of Our United Hearts lead the soul on the journey into union and immersion in the Divine Will. All that is needed is the soul's 'yes'. This 'yes' is your surrender to Our United Hearts." **(Jesus – March 12, 2017)**

Section 1. About the Apparitions 13

The Complete Image of the United Hearts

**Promises Concerning Reverence To
The Complete Image of the United Hearts**

1. "The souls who display this Image and regard it with reverence will receive, by the Hand of the Eternal Father, the grace to draw nearer to His Divine Will, even though the world separates itself more and more from His Eternal and Perfect Will."

2. "My Beloved Son vows the patronage of all the Heavenly Court to such souls who venerate this Image."

3. "Through the intercession of My Immaculate Heart, the souls devoted to this Image will be protected from heresy; thus, their Heavenly Mother will protect their Faith."

(Blessed Mother – May 24, 2009)

"Anywhere an Image of the Sacred Heart or the United Hearts is displayed receives Heaven's blessing. This is valuable information. You should display these Images in places of works, automobiles and every home – then, Heaven's blessing will always be with you."
(God the Father – June 1, 2020)

THE CHAMBERS OF THE UNITED HEARTS

"The Chambers of the United Hearts represent the various levels or depths that the soul embraces of God the Father's Will. So you see, the entire spiritual journey that Heaven has revealed here is a journey – beginning to end – into the Divine Will of God."
(St. Thomas Aquinas – June 27, 2006)

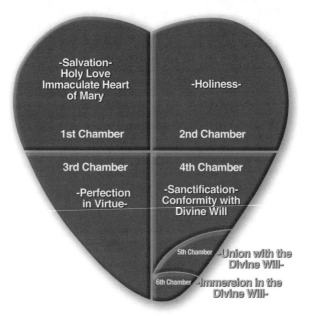

Section 1. About the Apparitions　　　　　　　　　　　　　　　　　　　15

"Never before have the Chambers of Our United Hearts been revealed to the world. Never before has such a spiritual journey been offered. Never before have I opened the depths of My Heart to such a degree to all humanity." **(Jesus – September 19, 2015)**

"The Father sends Me today to reiterate the importance of the United Hearts Revelation. The journey through the Chambers of Our United Hearts is the journey into union – even immersion – into the Divine Will of My Father. No other path has been given like it. The journey is a way of life – a commitment to personal holiness." **(Jesus – June 25, 2017)**

"You must accept the Truth I lay before you. Embrace it with your whole heart. Just as Holy Love is the light that shines through every virtue, this spiritual journey through the Chambers of the United Hearts is a well-lit path to personal holiness and sanctity which every soul will find himself upon in order to reach union with God. This journey is the Divine Will Itself. Therefore, the call to embrace this journey is not particular to race, creed, religious order or nationality; nor is it parochial to laity, clergy or religious. Indeed, it is for all people – all nations." **(St. Thomas Aquinas – August 3, 2004)**

"I tell you, no other Apparition has dealt so succinctly with personal holiness and the spiritual journey into the Sacred Heart of Jesus and the Immaculate Heart of Mary." **(St. Thomas Aquinas – October 2, 2013)**

Prayer to Propagate the Spirituality of the Chambers of the United Hearts

"Dear Blessed Mother, through the grace of Your Immaculate Heart, give me the courage to propagate the spirituality of the Chambers of the United Hearts through the spreading of these Messages. Help me to be Your instrument in the face of opposition so that this spirituality is perpetuated in generations to come. Amen."

(Jesus – September 8, 2007)

THE MESSAGES OF HOLY AND DIVINE LOVE

"This Mission and the Messages of Holy and Divine Love are the culmination of all the Messages Heaven has given to earth." **(Jesus – May 20, 2005)**

"Dear children, please treasure the journey you are given through these Messages. It is the missing link to all other Messages given to other visionaries. While many others deal with living in the Divine Will, the Journey through the Chambers of Our United Hearts gives you the way into the Divine Will. You cannot reach any destination without first making the journey." **(Mary, Refuge of Holy Love – May 10, 2017)**

"I am thankful for all who open their hearts to the many graces offered here – mainly the ever-deepening spiritual journey that these Messages offer." **(God the Father – November 23, 2017)**

"Appease My Most Sacred Heart and the Sorrowing Heart of My Mother by propagating the Messages of Holy and Divine Love." **(Jesus – September 16, 2011)**

MARANATHA SPRING AND SHRINE

"This prayer site is a property surrounded by grace – bordered with grace – saturated with grace. Of this, no one can explain away, rule against or in Truth, deny. While every effort has been made to prove otherwise, Heaven's grace remains – bearing witness to the source of the miracles here." **(Jesus – June 1, 2014)**

"No other mission or apparition site has been given so much – the Protectress of the Faith Devotion; the United Hearts Revelation and the spiritual journey through the Sacred Chambers therein, which lead to My Divine Will; the Revelation and Image of Mary, Refuge of Holy Love; and at last, the Revelation of the Mournful Heart of Jesus. A myriad of Messages have been imparted to the world here, as well as miraculous waters." **(God the Father – August 5, 2013)**

Section 1. About the Apparitions   17

"This property – more than any other apparition site – leads the soul to his salvation." **(God the Father – August 24, 2018)**

"This property continues to be a site of predilection for all people and all nations. There are few around the world now, as time draws on. The choicest graces pour out here. The inner recesses of My Heart open onto this property." **(Mary, Refuge of Holy Love – February 4, 2017)**

"Come to Me here at Heaven's site of predilection and allow Me to tenderly and compassionately tend to your needs." **(Blessed Mother – June 20, 2009)**

ECUMENICAL LAY APOSTOLATES

Over the years, Jesus and Blessed Mother have asked for the formation of various ecumenical lay apostolates to support and propagate the Holy Love Mission and Messages. These include:

- The Secular Order of Missionary Servants of Holy Love (1995)

- The Confraternity of the United Hearts (2000)

- The Children of the United Hearts (2012)

- The Lay Brothers of the United Hearts (2016)

- The Sisterhood of Divine Love (2016)

"Every one of My Apparitions and every true apostolate has carried with it the aim of living in the Divine Will. This is the ultimate underlying call and goal. The Chambers of the United Hearts is the master plan – the blueprint for every soul, every apostolate to follow." **(Blessed Mother – September 16, 2003)**

"I desire very much that apostolates and apparition sites do not oppose one another but, in Holy Love, assist each other in propagating My Messages to the world. I do not come to different sites to bring rivalry or friction but, everywhere and each time, to draw My children into My Immaculate Heart which is Holy Love. It is Satan who wants to divide and bring conflict to your midst. Then you are confused and do not see the oneness of My call to you."

"Dear, dear children, it is not for you to take pride in My coming to this site or any other. Each site that My Son sends Me to is continually and always a site of grace for all people. I never leave any of the sites I visit, but am always present there."

"Therefore, do not believe one Apparition is greater than another or that more grace is attendant to one than another. I come to you to bring reconciliation to the midst of your hearts, so that you will be reconciled to God and to each other. This – Holy Love – is the last hope of mankind." **(Our Lady of Guadalupe – August 12, 1996)**

MISSION STATEMENT

We are an ecumenical Ministry seeking personal holiness in and through the Message of Holy and Divine Love. We seek perfection through the Chambers of the United Hearts. We spread the Revelation of the Chambers of the United Hearts whenever and wherever we can, thus ushering in the triumphant victory of the United Hearts.

Section 2.
Pilgrimage Information

What is a Pilgrimage?

A pilgrimage is a journey to a sacred place undertaken as an act of religious devotion, either simply in order to venerate (honor) it, or to ask the fulfillment of some need, or as an act of penance or thanksgiving, or a combination of these.

I (Maureen) was telling Blessed Mother that I couldn't believe it was Fall already, and that She had brought us through another whole season of pilgrims and of tourists. Our Lady appeared, smiling. She said: *"Praise be to Jesus. I like how you put that – 'pilgrims and tourists.' There is a big difference, you know."*

"The pilgrim is here to draw deeper into the Chambers of Our United Hearts. He is here for his own holiness, to please God and to pray for others. The tourist, on the other hand, comes to inspect the site, to examine the exterior phenomena – sometimes to criticize."

"This Mission is about the interior life. The tourist misses the point. He is not that interested in the Messages or their meaning for himself. The pilgrim allows his heart to be transformed by Holy Love." (October 1, 2011)

Why make a Pilgrimage to Maranatha?

- **Mary, Refuge of Holy Love says**: *"I wish to tell the world why they should come to this apparition site."*
  - *"Jesus invites you."*
  - *"I invite you."*
  - *"You receive the Blessing of Truth here."*

- *"Your conscience is enlightened to see how you should improve in God's Eyes."*
- *"You receive an extra angel at Maranatha Spring to help you to live in Holy Love."*
- *"Many graces, healings and miracles abound here by Heaven's Hand."*

"These reasons to name a few should far outweigh any reason not to come." (March 13, 2016)

- **Our Lady of Lourdes says:** *"My Apparitions here are just as significant as My Apparitions in Lourdes. I told you, this is the Lourdes of this continent. Come with open hearts."* (February 11, 2017)

- **Mary, Refuge of Holy Love says:** *"The ordinary water at Maranatha Spring and in the lakes here have changed many hearts and healed many of physical difficulties by Heaven's Grace. My continual and abiding Presence on this property has transformed an ordinary soybean farm into a sacred refuge – a sanctuary of peace."* (April 8, 2017)

- **Padre Pio says:** *"There is no one who comes here that leaves without some type of healing – physical, spiritual or emotional. If they have a physical cross, it is either removed at the Spring, or they receive the grace to bear the cross of their affliction more admirably. This, in itself, is a healing. If the cross comes as an emotional affliction, the same is true. The cross is either removed or lightened. Therefore, let no one say, 'I came, but was not healed.' The same is true wherever Heaven meets earth – Lourdes, Fatima – all the great places of pilgrimage."* (September 30, 2006)

- **St. Thomas Aquinas says:** *"When people come to the shrine, they feel peace. That is because Our Lady's Heart, which is peace, has taken over the property, and Her Spirit is felt here. All of the objects on the property reflect this peace ...The water and objects carried away from this site carry with them the spirit of peace."* (September 21, 2006)

Section 2. Pilgrimage Information 21

- **Jesus says:** *"As you walk the property, you feel Heaven's peace. Many saints and angels accompany you, as well as My Mother and I Myself."* (June 8, 2012)

- **Mary, Refuge of Holy Love says:** *"I once again and always, invite all people and all nations to this prayer site to receive the Seal of Discernment and the Blessing of Truth. Without these special gifts, you are easily tricked into accepting evil as good."* (January 27, 2015)

- **Blessed Mother says:** *"Heaven offers you here a foretaste of being in the Presence of My Son, the angels and the saints, and Myself. Here at this site, I wrap My Arms around you. I keep your problems far distant from you. I offer you the solace of My Immaculate Heart. You are given the grace to begin or to deepen your journey through the Chambers of Our United Hearts. Each soul is given the grace of lasting peace if he opens his heart to the Seal of Discernment and understands what is most important – his own salvation."* (October 19, 2014)

- **Blessed Mother says:** *"I tell you, every grace attendant to this property comes into the world directly from the Heart of God the Father, which is pure Truth. Because every soul is called into the Heart of Truth and to live in Holy Truth, it follows every soul is called to come here."* (August 19, 2012)

- **Blessed Mother says:** *"Those of My children who step onto the property with <u>sincere hearts</u>, that is, a heart open to belief – not searching of reasons to disbelieve – will be plunged into the First Chamber of My Immaculate Heart and its Purifying Flame, as they receive the Seal of Discernment that My Son will place upon their foreheads. This anointing is a certain sign to Satan that you belong to Me, and that you are under Jesus' charge."* (March 22, 2013)

- **Our Lady of Lourdes says:** *"When souls come onto this prayer site, they will not only receive an illumination of* *conscience, but My Special Blessing, as well.* This Blessing, in the past, has been given in rare occasions here and at other apparition sites. What makes it 'special' is a special bond between the heart that receives it and My Own Immaculate Heart. For the soul to receive it, his heart must be open and receptive to the Messages and graces offered here."* (February 11, 2019)

*The next day, **Maureen asks:** *"Blessed Mother, does everyone who comes get both?"*

The Blessed Virgin Mary says: *"The illumination is given to those who come in humility, not in arrogance, trying to test the reality of these Apparitions and Messages. The same will be true of My Special Blessing. It is not right to test God."* (February 12, 2019)

• Once again, I see a Great Flame that I (Maureen) have come to know as the Heart of **God the Father**. This time there are sparks from the Flame falling on what looks to be the property of Holy Love. He says: *"The sparks you witness are representative of My Divine Will which falls upon the property and upon those who come here. Respect what I am telling you here today. All who come here are called."* (July 16, 2017)

• **Blessed Mother says:** *"This property brings souls to the threshold of the New Jerusalem. This is true, for the site itself embraces the Message of Holy Love. The Message is embraced by My Heart and is, in effect, the essence of My Immaculate Heart. My Immaculate Heart is the Gateway to the New Jerusalem. This is why special angels are given to those who come here. These angels assist in leading souls into the New Jerusalem; that is, across the threshold of My Heart."* (November 28, 2011)

• **Jesus says:** *"The pilgrim who comes to Maranatha will be satisfied in his needs. I have withheld nothing from those who come. I offer them the innermost Chambers of My Heart."* (May 3, 2001)

Section 2. Pilgrimage Information   23

PILGRIMAGE PREPARATION

Jesus says: *"See that often it is the effort put forth in the pilgrimage to come to the Shrine that bears much grace upon each one's arrival."* (July 13, 2001)

SPIRITUAL PREPARATION: Come in a prayerful mood. Many people pray and fast before their visit. Read or re-read about all the graces available on the property.

Instructions to Pilgrims

*   **Jesus says:** *"It is important for the pilgrims to know that their journey here is a pilgrimage, not a holiday. As such, they should prepare in advance with prayer and sacrifice so that their hearts are ready to receive the graces that are offered here."*

    "When they enter the property, they are offered the embrace of Our United Hearts. If their hearts are properly disposed, the embrace will prepare them for an illumination of conscience, as St. Michael's sword pricks their heart."

    "I desire that each pilgrim returns the embrace to Our United Hearts by living the Message of Holy and Divine Love in their own hearts. This, in itself, is all the recompense I ask."

    "With a heart full of love, accept any inconvenience that this journey presents. I speak not only of the journey here to this site, but the journey through the Chambers of Our United Hearts, as well."

    "You will please make this known." (March 27, 2006)

*   **St. Catherine of Siena says:** *"I wish to describe to you the proper disposition of heart for those who come to this apparition site, especially for the first time. Jesus desires that the heart of each pilgrim be open, that the heart be a blank page for Him to write upon. The less the pilgrim knows of others' opinions, the better. There are, as with every apparition site, many false rumors and false discernment attacking this place of Heaven's predilection."*

    "Jesus does not like people to come with preconceived

24   A Pilgrim's Guide to Maranatha Spring & Shrine

ideas of what may take place here. Therefore, do not anticipate any certain grace. Each one's pilgrimage is individual. Some may receive a profound illumination of conscience, others not."

"Do not look for proof of all that takes place here as being from Heaven. Do not come here to find fault. That is not discernment."

"Let your hearts be open to the individual experience that God has in store for you, knowing full well that Immaculate Mary invited you here to deepen your relationship with Her Son and God the Father. Allow the Spirit of Truth to carry you deeper into an intimate relationship with the Holy Trinity."

"Do not compare your experience here with anyone else's, for no two are alike. God knows best how to reach each heart. When you share your experiences, do so giving God the glory, for all grace comes from His Mercy and His Love. Never present yourself as being chosen or special or all-knowing in any way. Remember, humility is the first step on the Stairway to Holiness. There is a proper way to evangelize just as there is a proper way to do anything."

"Do not allow your heart to be filled with judgment against Heaven's efforts here. You do not gain merit in God's Eyes by opposing Him. You only invoke His Judgment. Such a one cooperates with evil."

"Make a sincere heartfelt 'Act of Contrition' before you come onto the property. Grace will then fill your heart." (April 24, 2008)

PHYSICAL PREPARATION: The miraculous Maranatha Spring has been given at this site. There is a manual outdoor water pump and you are encouraged to bring containers to fill and take home with you. Keep in mind you may need to walk a distance with the full containers, so it may be helpful to have wheeled carts to transport the containers.

Bring lawn chairs for outdoor Prayer Services. Also consider umbrellas for protection from either the sun or rain, and flashlights for evening services. Dress appropriately for the seasonal weather (rain, heat, snow).

Section 2. Pilgrimage Information 25

Bring cameras. Many miraculous pictures have been taken, particularly of the Sorrowful Mother statue at the Lake of Tears. Hearts are often found in nature and on photographs all around the property. *(See Appendix C.)*

Bring prayer petitions to touch to Our Lady's Blessing Point and place in the petition basket for Our Lady's intercession. You may also want to bring rosaries, medals, or other religious articles to touch to the Blessing Point.

TRAVEL / TRANSPORTATION

Maranatha Spring and Shrine is located in Eaton Township in eastern Lorain County, about 25 miles west of downtown Cleveland. Communities in the area include, alphabetically: Avon, Berea, Elyria, Fairview Park, Grafton, Independence, Middleburg Heights, North Olmsted, North Ridgeville, Oberlin, Olmsted Falls, Sheffield, Strongsville, and Westlake. Cleveland is in neighboring Cuyahoga County.

Please Note: All pilgrims are responsible for arranging their own travel and rental car arrangements, transportation to and from the Shrine, lodging and meals while visiting the Shrine.

**DRIVING DIRECTIONS TO
MARANATHA SPRING AND SHRINE**
37137 Butternut Ridge Road in Eaton Township
(Lorain County)

Please note that our 115-acre Shrine is physically located in Eaton Township in Lorain County, between the cities of North Ridgeville and Elyria. We use North Ridgeville's zip code (44039) for our mailing address. The Shrine is located on Butternut Ridge Road between Durkee Road and Route 83 (Avon Belden Road). It IS the far west end of Lorain Road (Lorain Road becomes Butternut Ridge Road west of Route 83). If you find a Butternut Ridge Road in another community or county, it will not lead to the Shrine. Taking

Lorain Road west from the Cleveland area, however, will always help you, and Lorain Road is well-known to local people.

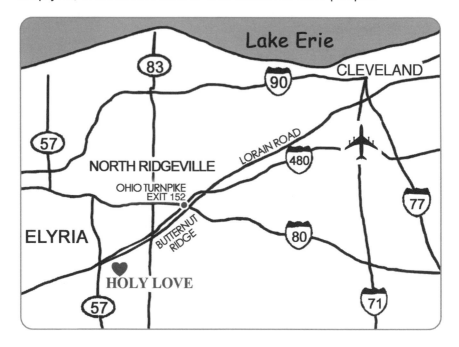

From the East and West

1. **From Ohio Turnpike (I-80).**
   Take **Exit 152** (10 West/North Ridgeville). After paying the toll, take Lorain Road West. This becomes Butternut Ridge Road. Maranatha Spring and Shrine will be on your left about 4 miles.

2. **From Interstate 90.**
   Take **Exit 153** – Avon/Avon Lake, Route 83. Travel south on Route 83 for 7.7 miles. Turn right (west) on Lorain Road which becomes Butternut Ridge Road when traveling west. Drive 1.5 miles. Maranatha Spring and Shrine will be on your left.

3. **From I-480 traveling west.**
   Take **Exit 2** (N. Ridgeville/Lorain Rd.) Travel west (left) on Lorain Road for 4.3 miles. *(Lorain Road becomes Butternut*

Section 2. Pilgrimage Information 27

Ridge Road in Eaton Township.) Maranatha Spring and Shrine will be on your left.

From the South

I-71 North to Route 82 West. Then take Route 83 North (right) to Lorain Road. Turn left (west) on Lorain Road, which becomes Butternut Ridge Road. Go about 1.5 miles. Maranatha Spring and Shrine will be on your left.

From the Northeast

TWO OPTIONS:

1. **I-90 to I-71 South to I-480 West.**
   Take **Exit 1** (left 2 lanes of I-480) onto Route 10. You do not get off the Interstate. I-480 turns into Route 10 at Exit 1.
   Continue west on Route 10 to Route 83 exit.
   At stop sign, make a left onto the overpass over the highway. At next stop sign, make a right onto Butternut Ridge Road. Shrine is 1.3 miles on your left.

2. **I-90 West to Route 83.**
   Take **Exit 153** (Exit sign says Avon Lake, North Ridgeville).
   Travel on Route 83 South for 7.7 miles.
   Turn right (west) at the stop light on Lorain Road, which becomes Butternut Ridge Road. Shrine is 1.5 miles on your left.

Approximate Mileage from Certain Cities			
Chicago IL	326	Lexington KY	310
Cincinnati OH	228	New York NY	470
Columbus OH	123	Philadelphia PA	425
Detroit MI	149	Pittsburgh PA	144
Toronto Canada 316			

TRANSPORTATION BY AIRPLANE / AMTRAK TRAIN / GREYHOUND BUS

CLEVELAND HOPKINS INTERNATIONAL AIRPORT

5300 Riverside Drive   Cleveland, Ohio 44135
Airport Information   216-265-6030
www.clevelandairport.com

(There are numerous hotels that provide shuttle services to travelers.)

Driving Directions to the Shrine

(The Shrine is approximately 15 miles west of the Airport)

1. Follow the signs for **I-480 West**. (*Left out of Airport on Route 237 North. Bear right to Brookpark Road. Left at light on Brookpark Road. Right at light on Grayton Road to I-480 West on your left*).
2. Take **Exit 2 – Lorain Road**.* At the bottom of the exit ramp, turn left traveling west. Go four miles. Maranatha Spring and Shrine is on your left.
Lorain Road becomes Butternut Ridge Road.

www.amtrak.com
800-USA-RAIL | 800-872-7245
Nearest Station: Elyria
410 E. River Rd

www.greyhound.com
800-231-2222
Nearest Station: Elyria

Please Note: *Pilgrims will need to arrange their own transportation from the above terminals.*

LODGING

AREA HOTELS, MOTELS AND CAMPGROUNDS

For a current list of area hotels, motels and campgrounds, visit our website at holylove.org or email us at MAMSHL@holylove.org or

Section 2. Pilgrimage Information 29

call the Shrine at 440-327-8006 ext. 222.

Call the 800 number of your favorite hotel chain for reservations. Some local hotels offer special rates for pilgrims visiting the Shrine. Be sure to identify yourself as a pilgrim to receive the special rates. Some hotels offer shuttle service to/from the Cleveland Hopkins International Airport.

Communities in the area include, alphabetically: Avon, Berea, Cleveland, Elyria, Fairview Park, Grafton, Independence, Middleburg Heights, North Olmsted, North Ridgeville, Oberlin, Olmsted Falls, Sheffield, Strongsville, and Westlake.

(Pilgrims are responsible for arranging their own transportation to and from their hotels/motels and to and from the Shrine.)

LORAIN COUNTY VISITORS BUREAU
Phone: 800-334-1673   www.visitloraincounty.com

CHAMBERS OF COMMERCE

Lorain County	440-328-2550	Oberlin	440-774-6262
North Olmsted	440-777-3368	Strongsville	440-238-3366
North Ridgeville	440-327-3737	Westlake	440-835-8787

NATIONAL WEATHER SERVICE
Phone: 216-265-2370   www.weather.gov

FREQUENTLY ASKED QUESTIONS

1. Is the Shrine just for Catholics?
This is an <u>ecumenical</u> Shrine. Heaven is inviting all people of all faiths from all nations to come here, including, but not limited to, Catholics.

2. When is the best time to make a pilgrimage?

Pilgrims visit the Shrine throughout the year, but especially during the spring, summer and fall. The Feast of Mary, Refuge of Holy Love (May 5th), the Feast of the United Hearts (Sunday after the Feast of the Immaculate Heart), Blessed Mother's Birthday (August 5th), and the Feast of God the Father and His Divine Will (first Sunday in August) are special grace-filled times to visit. Thousands of pilgrims visit the Shrine during special events held throughout the year.

LOCAL WEATHER *(Degrees Fahrenheit)*								
Month	Avg. High	Avg. Low	Month	Avg. High	Avg. Low	Month	Avg. High	Avg. Low
Jan	34	21	May	70	50	Sep	74	56
Feb	37	24	Jun	79	60	Oct	62	45
Mar	47	30	Jul	83	64	Nov	51	37
Apr	59	40	Aug	81	63	Dec	38	26

3. Where is the closest airport?

The closest airport is the **Cleveland Hopkins International Airport**, located approximately 18 miles east of the Shrine. Most major airlines fly to this airport *(see Transportation)*. The **Akron-Canton Regional Airport** is located approximately 58 miles southeast of the Shrine in North Canton:

Cleveland Hopkins International Airport (CLE)
Information: 216-265-6030   www.clevelandairport.com

Akron-Canton Regional Airport
Information: 888-434-2359   www.akroncantonairport.com

4. Where will we stay? Is overnight camping allowed?

There are numerous hotels and motels, bed and breakfasts, and campgrounds within driving distance from the Shrine. No lodging is available at or adjacent to the Shrine and the Shrine does not allow any overnight camping or motor homes parked on the property overnight. *(See also the Lodging section.)*

Section 2. Pilgrimage Information 31

5. How do we arrange for a group to visit the Shrine by bus?
If you would like to organize a bus group, please contact us for assistance (440-327-8006 Ext. 222). Bus groups are responsible for coordinating their own travel arrangements, transportation, lodging and meals. Group leaders should contact us at least two weeks prior to the desired pilgrimage date(s), so we can properly accommodate the group.

6. Are tours given?
The Shrine does not conduct tours. Please visit our Welcome Center for a brief orientation and to pick up a copy of our free Visitor's Guide (available in both English and Spanish) containing a map and description of all shrines and places of interest on the grounds.

7. What are the Shrine hours? *(Subject to change.)*
The Shrine is open to the public 365 days a year. On certain holidays, the grounds close at 5 PM and the buildings may be closed. Call the Ministry's phone line (440-327-8006) or check our website (holylove.org) for seasonal hours. In case of inclement weather, announcements about Shrine closings and/or canceled service(s) are posted on the Ministry's phone line.

8. Is there a dress code?
The Shrine is a sacred place, so we encourage visitors to show due respect by dressing comfortably, but modestly. Please do not wear clothing such as halter tops, short shorts, swimsuits, mini- or micro-mini skirts, see-through clothing, or any clothing with offensive wording and/or designs.

9. Are meals available at the Shrine?
No food service is available at the Shrine, but there are many restaurants in the area. The cafeteria has vending machines with drinks and snacks. Outdoor picnic tables are available, but no grilling and/or open fires are allowed. Groups may arrange to have catered meals delivered to the Shrine. Food service may be available in the cafeteria during special events.

10. Are alcohol and/or smoking allowed?
Pilgrims may not partake of any alcohol or illegal substances while

visiting the property. All of the shrine buildings are smoke-free.

11. How much walking is involved?
Pilgrims are encouraged to walk the grounds, if physically able. Many of the shrines on this 115-acre property are only accessible on foot or by golf cart, such as St. Michael's Shrine and all of the shrines in the Field of the United Hearts.

12. Are wheelchairs and/or golf carts available?
Pilgrims should bring their own wheelchairs or arrange to rent them from their hotel or nearby pharmacies. Call 440-327-8006 ext. 222 for information about golf cart rentals.

13. Can we bring our pets?
Pets are not permitted on the grounds beyond the bridge at the entrance. Pilgrims traveling with pets are asked to leave their pet(s) in their vehicle in a safe manner as they visit the shrines.

14. Will our group meet with the Visionary?
The Visionary spends a great deal of time in prayer and is not available to meet with groups of pilgrims or to give talks to groups.

15. When are Prayer Services held?
Call our Ministry phone line or visit our website for information concerning our daily prayer services and announcements about special feast day celebrations and/or special events. Prayer Services may also be livestreamed on our website.

16. Will there be an Apparition during the Service?
When the Visionary is present at a Prayer Service, there may be an Apparition. When our Heavenly Guest(s) arrive, it will be announced. If you can kneel, please do so, while the Message is given to the Visionary. We will be told when the Blessing is being given. The prayers then continue. The Message is then read at the end of the service.

"When I appear – not only here, but anywhere – I speak to all the angels of the people present, while I appear and speak to the visionary or visionaries. I guide these angels

Section 2. Pilgrimage Information 33

as to the welfare of those in their charge. It is up to each individual to open his heart to Heavenly inspiration during or directly after each Apparition. Be open to My Sovereignty. At the same time, realize that during these present moments – during or directly after an Apparition – Satan tries to mislead and interfere. This is the reason, My dear, dear children, you should pray for discernment before an Apparition and after this grace-filled event. " (Blessed Mother – August 23, 2012)

17. **Are pilgrims allowed to pray over or lay hands on other pilgrims?**
It is our policy and Our Lady's request that <u>no one prays over another</u>. Our Lady has promised all the graces pilgrims need when they come to Her Shrine with open and sincere hearts.

18. **Is swimming or immersion in the lakes permitted?**
All of the waters on the property have graces of healing and conversion, but swimming and/or immersion in the lakes are <u>NOT</u> permitted. Instead, Jesus has given a special prayer to recite whenever any water from this property is used in making the *Sign of the Cross.* To obtain the graces, bless yourself with the lake water while making the *Sign of the Cross (In the Name of the Father, and of the Son, and of the Holy Spirit. Amen.)* and reciting the prayer below. Pilgrims are welcome to bring containers to take lake water home with them.

19. **How do we use the Maranatha Spring water?**
Bless yourself with the Spring water while making the *Sign of the Cross* and reciting the following special prayer.

Prayer to be Recited Whenever Any Water from this Property is Used in Making the Sign of the Cross

"Dear Jesus, as I bless myself with this water, open my heart to the grace Heaven desires I have. Let me look into my soul with the eyes of Truth. Give me the <u>courage</u> and <u>humility</u> to do so. Heal me according to the Will of Your Father. Amen."
(Jesus – January 18, 2008)

20. How much Maranatha water are we allowed to take home?
Bring your own containers and take as much water as you can manage, keeping in mind any airport restrictions for those traveling by plane.

21. Where can we buy books and religious articles?
Please visit the **United Hearts Gift Shop in the Aquinas Center.** For information, please call 440-327-4532, or visit our online website at **www.RosaryoftheUnborn.com**.

Glossary of Frequently Used Terms

Apparition – A certain kind of supernatural vision in which something naturally invisible is seen with the bodily eye.

Feast Day – A special day set apart for the liturgical commemoration of Our Lord, The Holy Trinity, Our Lady, Angels or Saints, or an important religious event.

Graces – A supernatural gift of God to an intellectual creature.

Holy Water – Water blessed by a priest according to the form in the *"Rituale Romanum."* It is a sacramental.

Locutions – Words heard by the ear, but produced supernaturally.

Shrine – A sacred image in a church, house, on land, or elsewhere to which special devotion is accorded. A holy place to which pilgrimages are made.

Venerate – Does not mean "to worship" or "pray to." Rather, it does mean to pay honor to a saint in Heaven (e.g., Blessed Mother) who, when asked in prayer, will by their intercession and their own example of sanctification, help the faithful on earth to grow in Christian virtue and holiness. Venerating the saints does not detract from the glory given only to God in worship, since whatever good they possess is a total gift from God's bounty of graces.

Visionary – A person who receives supernatural perceptions.

Section 3.
Journey of Holiness

ENTRANCE TO MARANATHA SPRING AND SHRINE

"Every soul that enters this property is embraced by the United Hearts and receives the grace for conversion in that present moment." *(Jesus – March 26, 2006)*

"When you step onto the property it is as though time stands still and you are enfolded in God's grace." *(Mary, Refuge of Holy Love – August 21, 2015)*

"As you enter this property and receive with <u>sincere hearts</u> the Seal of Discernment, so too, you receive the sincere desire for personal holiness through the journey of Our United Hearts." *(Jesus – June 9, 2014)*

"I will offer My Blessing of Truth to all who come with a <u>sincere heart</u>. This Blessing will reveal self-knowledge to the soul to deepen his spiritual journey into the Chambers of Our United Hearts." *(Jesus – September 17, 2014)*

"Make a sincere, heartfelt **Act of Contrition** *before you come onto the property. Grace will then fill your heart."* *(St. Catherine of Siena – April 24, 2008)*

Act of Contrition
O my God, I am heartily sorry for having offended Thee, and I detest all my sins, because I dread the loss of Heaven and the pains of hell; but most of all because they offend Thee, my God, Who art all good and deserving of all my love. I firmly resolve, with the help of Thy grace, to confess my sins, to do penance, and to amend my life. Amen.

"Here, child, is a prayer I desire all who journey in pilgrimage to the prayer site, recite:"

Prayer to be Recited by Visiting Pilgrims
"Dear Heavenly Mother, I know You have called me to this place of Your favor for Your purpose. As I step onto the property You have chosen as Your own, help me to realize that You are inviting me into a deeper personal conversion through the Revelation of the United Hearts. Help me to begin this journey by stepping into Your Heart which is Holy Love."

"If You, Blessed Mother, look into my heart and see that I am unprepared or unwilling to take this first step, extend Your Hand filled with grace towards me and I will take it."

"Do not allow me, Your child, to pass up this opportunity through doubts or pride. If I came here only looking for error, take this spirit of arrogance away, dear Mother. I desire to be Yours in this present moment through Holy Love. Amen."
(Jesus – May 22, 2004)

Section 3. Journey of Holiness 37

MAKING THE JOURNEY OF HOLINESS

Our Lady Describes the Layout of Her 115-Acre Shrine

"Please understand, My children, that **the layout of this property represents the soul's journey into holiness and Our United Hearts.**

1. The soul is first drawn into My Sorrowful and Immaculate Heart (represented at the **Lake of Tears**), where he is purged of many of his most flagrant faults.

2. Then he travels along guided by the angels – as is represented on the property by the **Lake of Angels**.

3. He receives many graces to move deeper into My Heart and into Divine Love, the Heart of My Son. This is represented by **Maranatha Spring** on the property.

4. Finally, in conformity to the Divine Will of God, he arrives at the **Field of Victory, Our United Hearts and the Triumph**.

5. Understand that every triumph and victory is surrounded by the Way of the Cross. And thus you have at the back of the property – the **Stations of the Cross**."
(Our Lady – December 12, 1999)

"Maranatha is Aramaic for 'Come, Lord Jesus'."
(Our Lady – November 27, 1993)

(Pilgrims are encouraged to walk the grounds in a spirit of pilgrimage. Maximum driving speed is 10 mph. Please see the Shrine map on the back cover for the location of each numbered shrine.)

1 THE SORROWFUL MOTHER SHRINE AND LAKE OF TEARS

"My dear children, this will be known as THE LAKE OF TEARS, and many promises will bear fruit here. Manifest will be My Grace. You do not see the fullness and the entirety of My plan, but much of it hinges on this humble little shrine that Heaven has chosen for this site." *(Our Lady – August 8, 1997)*

"Please ask the people to ask Jesus to forgive them any lack of love in their hearts as they approach the Spring and Lake of Tears." *(Our Lady of Guadalupe – November 12, 1997)*

"The Shrine of your Heavenly Mother's Sorrows will be a site of favor. The water coming into the Lake of Tears is My Tears. This water will bring special consolation to mothers who sorrow for their wayward children. For today, it is the good who suffer and the converted who are persecuted. I understand the pain of a mother's heart and I have requested this grace from My Beloved Son."

"Continually there are many angels in attendance with Me at this Lake of Tears. They are carrying petitions to Heaven as I desire. You will begin to see many images there. My affection and Presence is always at Maranatha Spring, the Lake of Tears and the holy Stations of the Cross. Indeed, I am present everywhere on this chosen property. I am praying with you and for you." *(The Sorrowful Mother – September 8, 1997)*

Section 3. Journey of Holiness   39

"The Shrine of your Mother's Sorrows is predestined as a place of great favor. I invite every nation to come and to join Me there in prayer. All issues can be resolved through Holy Love. It is here I will show favor upon those who listen and respond. Give to Me your hearts and I will give to you My Grace. Place your petitions at My Feet and I will respond to them according to God's Divine Will. You have not chosen Me; I have chosen you. Here I will unite your hearts to My own Sorrowful and Immaculate Heart. The greatest hour of My Grace is at hand. I have come to share with you God's Eternal Plan. It is here I will bless you." *(Our Lady – September 15, 1997)*

"Please make it known that My consolation and My Grace are attendant to the Lake of Tears, and that this is the way to peace and reconciliation of hearts in the world." *(The Sorrowful Mother – September 15, 1997 / Dedication of Our Lady of Sorrows Shrine)*

"At my Lake of Tears I will alleviate the afflicted, make steadfast the wavering heart, and console the downtrodden." *(Our Lady of Grace – September 16, 1997)*

"My daughter, the course of My Mission is going to change, for many will come to see the certain sign I left at the Lake of Tears last night. The face on My Image there will be viewed by many (not all) as alive and vibrant – flesh-toned. This will be photographed; but when My children move close to the Image it will appear as any statue; from a distance they will see My Skin, which will draw them closer." *(Mary, Refuge of Holy Love – December 12, 1999 / Feast of Our Lady of Guadalupe)*

"Jesus says that those souls who come on pilgrimage to the property, and prayerfully visit the Shrine of My Sorrows or the Stations of the Cross, and also pray the *Consecration of the Heart of the World to Our United Hearts*, will receive the *Complete Blessing of Our United Hearts*." *(Blessed Mother – May 16, 2012)*

*(See page 81 for the Promises attendant to
the United Hearts Blessing.)*

The Consecration of the Heart of the World to the United Hearts

"*Most Compassionate United Hearts of the Most Holy Trinity and the Immaculate Heart of Mary*, accept this, my prayer, on behalf of the heart of the world. Awaken the heart of the world to the Truth of the difference between good and evil."

"Inspire each soul to consecrate their hearts and their lives to the United Hearts; thereby strengthening the heart of the world in this resolve."

"We beg You, dear United Hearts, pour the grace of Your Inspiration into the heart of the world, strengthening it in Truth and in Holy Love. In this Heavenly Inspiration, draw the heart of the world into union with the Will of God. Amen."

(Blessed Mother – May 10, 2012)

THE SORROWFUL MOTHER MEDITATIONS

1. First Sorrow of Mary
The Prophecy of Simeon
"I invite you to meditate upon My knowledge of all future Sorrow which was given to Me by God at the Presentation."
Present-Day Sorrow
"Hearts of unbelievers – most especially those who propagate error."
Our Father...   Hail Mary...   All Glory Be...

2. Second Sorrow of Mary
The Flight Into Egypt
"I invite you to meditate upon the anxiety in the hearts of Joseph and Myself for the safety of Baby Jesus, and the anxiety I feel today for those who run from salvation."

Section 3. Journey of Holiness   41

Present-Day Sorrow
"Misuse of authority – politically or ecclesiastically."
Our Father...   Hail Mary...   All Glory Be...

3. **Third Sorrow of Mary**
   The Loss of the Child Jesus in the Temple
   "I invite you to meditate upon the pain of separation I felt when Jesus was lost. This is a pain all should feel when they separate themselves from My Son through sin."
   ### Present-Day Sorrow
   "Disrespect for human life from conception to natural death."
   Our Father...   Hail Mary...   All Glory Be...

4. **Fourth Sorrow of Mary**
   The Meeting of Jesus and Mary
   on the Way of the Cross
   "I invite you to meditate upon the pain of My Heart as I saw the physical pain My Son suffered due to lack of love in hearts. Also think of the pain I suffer today for lack of love in hearts."
   ### Present-Day Sorrow
   "The obtuse conscience of the heart of the world in discernment of sin, and the difference between good and evil."
   Our Father...   Hail Mary...   All Glory Be...

5. **Fifth Sorrow of Mary**
   The Crucifixion
   "I invite you to meditate upon the pain of a Mother's Heart at the death of Her Son, and the virtue of forgiveness I received through grace and prayer. Think of My pain at the sight of the death of the unborn."
   ### Present-Day Sorrow
   "Lack of respect for personal holiness."
   Our Father...   Hail Mary...   All Glory Be...

6. **Sixth Sorrow of Mary**
   The Taking Down of the Body of Jesus from the Cross
   "I invite you to meditate upon the acceptance of Divine Will that I surrendered to. Ask for that same grace in your life now."
   Present-Day Sorrow
   "Neglect of love of God and neighbor."
   Our Father... Hail Mary... All Glory Be...

7. **Seventh Sorrow of Mary**
   The Burial of Jesus
   "I invite you to meditate upon the understanding I had, as My Son was placed in the tomb, that death was a beginning and not an end. Think of the extreme sorrow I felt as I cleansed His Wounds. My sorrow was, as it is today, for the lack of love in hearts."
   Present-Day Sorrow
   "Mankind's indifference towards his own salvation."
   Our Father... Hail Mary... All Glory Be...

   (Our Lady – September 5, 1997 and September 15 & 18, 2011)

❷ OUR LADY AT THE ARBOR

(Our Lady appeared above the Arbor from May 30, 2004 – June 19, 2004)

"I desire that My Image be placed on top of the Arbor. The Arbor represents the bridge of Holy Love that God desires between Heaven and earth. I am blessing each one who comes to the Arbor." *(Our Lady at the Arbor – 6:00 p.m. June 5, 2004)*

"The people will continue to photograph Me here (at the Arbor)." *(Blessed Mother – May 30, 2004)*

Section 3. Journey of Holiness   43

"I am not leaving you, My children. I will always look down upon you at this grace-filled area. Make My Immaculate Heart your shrine for My Heart is always with you." *(Our Lady at the Arbor 6:00 P.M. – June 19, 2004)*

> **Prayer of Perfection in the Virtuous Life**
> *"Dear Immaculate Heart of Mary, Protectress of Faith and Defender of All Virtue, Refuge of Holy Love,* take my heart and place it under Your Maternal gaze."
> "Protect the virtues I am seeking to perfect. Help me to recognize any weakness in virtue and to overcome it. I surrender my virtuous life to Your charge. Amen."
> *(Jesus – September 9, 2011)*
>
> **Prayer to be Virtuous Today**
> *"Dear Jesus, through the Immaculate Heart of Mary,* open my heart to the grace I need to be perfected in virtue today in every present moment. Amen."
> *(Jesus – March 10, 2003)*

 LAKE OF THE HOLY ANGELS

"I have come to confirm to you that around the Lake of Angels Jesus has ordained that one from each choir of angels will stand in attendance. Many graces will be given. Faith will be protected and Satan's snares will be revealed to souls. I, Myself, will reign over this lake and many graces will be forthcoming." *(Our Lady – April 3, 1999)*

"I have come to tell you that the myriads of angels who attend this prayer site stand ready to welcome each soul who comes here." *(Angel Alanus – June 6, 2011)*

"Thousands upon thousands of angels are present here on this property. They often appear as glittering lights. Ask them to assist you." *(Angel Alanus – November 7, 2011)*

"I invite each of you to give thanks for the action of the angels and saints in your lives daily and here at this property." *(Jesus – October 31, 2014)*

> **Invocation to the Holy Angels**
> *"Dear Heavenly Angels,* all who reside in Heaven and assist us on earth, guide us. Minister to the needs of all mankind. Be for us a liaison between God and man. Protect the tabernacles of the world as you protect our hearts as well, against the attacks of the evil one. Dear angels, take all our needs and petitions to Heaven and lay them on the Divine Altar of the Sacred Heart of Jesus. Amen."
> *(December 31, 1995)*

 CHAPEL OF THE HOLY ANGELS

(In this Chapel are found inspirational testimonials given by many pilgrims.)

"There is a multitude of angels at this apparition site – each one with a specific duty towards the salvation of souls ... There is an angel at the House of Testimonies whose job is to inspire those who read the testimonies." *(Blessed Mother – August 2, 2009)*

"The angels attendant to this property are present to assist those who come along the path of personal holiness. They are eager to help, and often do. Their assistance is most often in the background and goes unnoticed. What seems mundane may suddenly become a significant grace – something that leads the soul into the Chambers of the United Hearts."

"The angels open the 'eyes' of the heart to see what they did not see a moment before. After such graces are experienced, it is

Section 3. Journey of Holiness   45

the angels who invoke *'Mary, Protectress of the Faith'* so that what is given so freely will not be taken away through Satan's doubts."

"Even if unknowing, unbelievers and detractors come here, the angels are doing their work in the background. The soul does not have to see us for us to work towards his holiness. The angels continually pray that souls will be responsive to grace. Without the positive action of free will, the work of every angel is negated." *(Angel Alanus – November 9, 2011)*

> **A Prayer of Invocation to the Angels**
> *"Dear Servants of God, Angel Guardians,* invoke Jesus to awaken each soul as to the path he follows. Bring each soul to the fullness of his faith. We ask this, dear Jesus, through your Servant Angels and the Protectress of Our Faith. Amen."

 GOD THE FATHER SHRINE

Established 2013

Established 2020

"I will place Paternal Joy in the hearts of those who step into My little shrine for the first time, so long as their hearts are open. Even when the structure may be increased in size, My Paternal Blessing of Joy will be there, as My Blessing is not attendant to a structure, but is part of My Divine Will." (God the Father – May 1, 2019)

"The Blessing will be given once to suffice the rest of the soul's life." (God the Father – April 17, 2019)

"My Paternal Blessing of Joy ... will place repentance in the heart of the unrepentant." (God the Father – June 1, 2019)

Spiritual Baptism of the Unborn

"Almighty God, Father, Son, and Holy Spirit, Your Power and Grace transcends all time and space. Cast now Your compassionate glance upon all life in the womb from the moment of conception until the moment of birth. Caress these innocent souls in Your Merciful Love. Protect this life from any marauder. Bestow upon each soul You create a spiritual baptism, in Your Name, Father, Son, and Holy Spirit. Amen."
(Our Lady – May 16, 1996)

Prayer to Recognize God's Omnipotence

"Lord God, make Your Power known to me today in every situation."
(God the Father – January 17, 2018)

 ## ST. MICHAEL SHRINE AND LAKE

"The time is coming when I will appear on the site and establish a respite of prayer for rebellious souls. There, parents of wayward children will find peace. Even the most reluctant souls will find their way back to the Heart of Jesus through petitions laid at My Feet in this most precious area of the property. Most of all, priests will find their way back to the true Tradition of Faith." *(St. Michael the Archangel – September 1, 2003)*

"St. Michael's Lake has been set aside to hold special blessings for the Remnant, for he is the vanguard of a new era. Come and partake of the blessings, and be strengthened in the Truth." *(Blessed Mother – October 9, 2005)*

Section 3. Journey of Holiness   47

"I am the Vanguard of Victory in every battle against the Dragon. God desires my Shield of Truth be placed over every heart, and in His Final Victory – over the heart of the world. Therefore, I stand guard over this property by my lake. The Heavenly Peace you feel here is under my protection. I extend my Shield of Truth to all who visit me here." *(St. Michael the Archangel – September 29, 2014)*

St. Michael's Shield of Truth Prayer

"St. Michael, you are our defender and safeguard against evil. Place your Shield of Truth over us and defend us in the battle which Satan wages against Truth. Help us to see the righteous path of Holy Love."

"Clarify our choices between good and evil by placing us always behind your Shield of Truth. Amen."

(St. Michael the Archangel – March 14, 2006)

Prayer for the Conversion of the Heart of the World

"Heavenly Father, Creator of the Universe, place over the heart of the world St. Michael's Shield of Truth. In so doing, convict the hearts of those far from You, dear Father, to pursue personal holiness by living in Holy Love. Help every soul to live in the Truth of Holy Love. Amen."

(St. Michael the Archangel – December 15, 2010)

7 MEMORIAL TO THE UNBORN

"The silent victims of abortion grieve My Heart very much. They are the victims of compromised Truth and abusive authority. They cannot defend themselves or speak for themselves. They will never have the opportunity to develop the talents and strengths God gave them." *(Mary, Refuge of Holy Love – July 8, 2016)*

> **Spiritual Baptism of the Unborn**
> *"Almighty God, Father, Son, and Holy Spirit, Your Power and Grace transcends all time and space. Cast now Your compassionate glance upon all life in the womb from the moment of conception until the moment of birth. Caress these innocent souls in Your Merciful Love. Protect this life from any marauder. Bestow upon each soul You create a spiritual baptism, in Your Name, Father, Son, and Holy Spirit. Amen."*
> *(Our Lady – May 16, 1996)*

 ## INTERNATIONAL SHRINE OF THE WHITE MADONNA

The ecclesial movement of the Armata Bianca ("White Army") started in the city of L'Aquila, Italy for the sole purpose of ending abortion in the world, and has since grown internationally. Holy Love Ministries has been honored as a recipient of the White Madonna ("Mary, Mother of the Unborn") because of its ongoing pro-life efforts, especially through the Rosary of the Unborn. We are grateful for the privilege of hosting Our Lady's International Shrine.

"This rosary *(Jesus is holding the Rosary of the Unborn – See Appendix A for Heaven's promises and how to pray it)* is like pure gold from Heaven and should be distributed around the world with the White Madonna." *(Jesus – September 17, 2004)*

"Babies who are aborted receive a baptism of blood and they always choose the light when they see it and are saved." *(Jesus – July 6, 2002)*

Section 3. Journey of Holiness 49

"You (mankind) have chosen to abort sound leadership, righteous leadership. You have aborted those who would have been priests, Bishops, Cardinals and even a Pope. You have killed in the womb those, who long ago, would have found cures for cancer, aids and many genetic disorders. You have done this all in the name of freedom." *(Blessed Mother – January 22, 2015)*

Chaplet of the Unborn
(See Appendix A for the Promises for praying the Chaplet)

1. "The recognition by all that God creates human life at the moment of conception."
   Our Father... Hail Mary... Hail Mary... Hail Mary...

2. "An end to all legalized abortion."
   Our Father... Hail Mary... Hail Mary... Hail Mary...

3. "For all expectant mothers – that they value the precious life within them."
   Our Father... Hail Mary... Hail Mary... Hail Mary...

4. "The conviction of conscience in the Truth for anyone considering abortion."
   Our Father... Hail Mary... Hail Mary... Hail Mary...

5. "An inner healing for all who have been involved in any way with abortion:
   • Mothers and Fathers
   • Health Caregivers
   • Legislators
   • Those who, in their thoughts, words, actions or lack of action, have supported abortion."
   Our Father... Hail Mary... Hail Mary... Hail Mary...

"At the end, say the following prayer:"
"Heavenly Father, please forgive this generation for the arrogance of abortion. Heal the many wounds abortion has caused in our hearts, in the world and in our relationship with You. Unite us in the Truth. Amen."
(Blessed Mother – March 24, 2013)

FIELD OF THE UNITED HEARTS
(Field of Victory)

"Where angels pray and play" (BVM '21)

"The United Hearts Field on our property here is always the field of the Holy Angels, as well. It is a place where joys and triumphs meet trials and sorrows – where peace washes over conflict. Desire to be there – not just for an Apparition, but whenever you are faced with doubts, confusion or conflict. It is in this holy place Truth reigns – Truth which never changes to suit human reason."

"It is here the soul will cease to grapple with Satan's lies. The Holy Angels are there always – waiting for each soul who finds his way there. Their peace will be with those who come in faith. The Angels bear Truth always. They are My Messengers. They are the emissaries of the United Hearts." *(God the Father – October 2, 2021 / Feast of the Guardian Angels)*

"I desire that My children come to know the Field of the United Hearts as a place of My favor and a destination of pilgrimages. I will welcome all who come with My Blessing of Holy Love." *(Our Lady – February 14, 1996)*

Victory Prayer
"Heavenly Father, I *(Name)*, desire to be Your humble instrument in bringing about the Victory of the United Hearts. I understand that this Victory will be a Victory of Your Divine Will through Holy and Divine Love. I wish to be a part of that Victory now, by living in Your Will in this present moment. I embrace the crosses You give me, for I know they are my strength in the journey towards Your Victory in my heart. Remind me, Heavenly Father, that Your Victory will be ours, as well. It will be a Triumph of Love. Help me to be Your Love in the world. Amen."
(Jesus – June 19, 2007)

Section 3. Journey of Holiness   51

9 MARANATHA SPRING

"Joyfully, I reveal to you today that the waters of Maranatha are as the Lourdes of this continent. They are comparable in healing grace, both in body and soul. They are much like the Cascade in Betania. Therefore, you can propagate it with much faith and hope." *(Our Lady – May 31, 1995)*

"The abundance of grace that will flow from My Spring will reveal truths, heal, and bring peace. But no grace will be so great as the numbers who will find conversion." *(Our Lady – May 2, 1994)*

"I am continually present and awaiting all mankind at Maranatha Spring. It is here I will comfort and console those who come to Me. I desire, as My Son allows, to alleviate afflictions and render certain and untold grace. Ask My children to surrender their petitions to Me at the Spring." *(Our Lady – August 18, 1996)*

"Please ask the people to ask Jesus to forgive them any lack of love in their hearts as they approach the Spring and Lake of Tears." *(Our Lady of Guadalupe – November 12, 1997)*

"Before My Son returns, each soul will be made to know his state before God. Many await anxiously this hour of enlightenment. But, My dear children, you do not need to wait. Come to My site of favor. Step onto the property. Taste of My Spring. Your consciences will be laid bare before you. All that impedes your journey of Holy Love will be shown you."
"This is a favor, given with such force and strength at this site; it remains unprecedented elsewhere. You may travel and search for such grace; but it is here, now." *(Our Lady – July 10, 1998)*

"On the property here, <u>the angel that is assigned each soul at Maranatha Spring</u> tries to bring the peace of Holy Love into the soul he is assigned. The angel tries to inspire the Message of Holy Love to come alive in the heart of the soul, no matter his faith, creed or lack thereof." *(Mary of the Holy Angels – August 2, 2009)*

"The water and objects carried away from this site carry with them the spirit of peace." *(St. Thomas Aquinas – September 21, 2006)*

"You can carry the water from Maranatha Spring with you as protection." *(Blessed Mother – November 8, 2013)*

"At Lourdes I asked for penance. Here I ask for penance, prayer and sacrifice. I give you here a Spring, as well. It is the Lourdes of this hemisphere – just as powerful and miraculous as the one so far away in France." *(Our Lady of Lourdes – February 11, 2016)*

"The ordinary water at Maranatha Spring and in the lakes here have changed many hearts and healed many of physical difficulties by Heaven's Grace." *(Mary, Refuge of Holy Love – April 8, 2017)*

"When anyone blesses himself with Maranatha Spring water, he is immediately surrounded by a myriad of angels." *(St. Michael the Archangel – March 16, 2017)*

Prayer to be Recited Whenever Any Water from this Property is Used in Making the Sign of the Cross
"Dear Jesus, as I bless myself with this water, open my heart to the grace Heaven desires I have. Let me look into my soul with the eyes of Truth. Give me the courage and humility to do so. Heal me according to the Will of Your Father. Amen."

"It is not necessary that the water be blessed prior to its use in this way by a priest. Heaven releases many graces at this Site and with this water."
(Jesus – January 18, 2008)

Section 3. Journey of Holiness

10 UNITED HEARTS SHRINE

"Dear children, thank you for persevering and developing this shrine. Many will come here, and lives and hearts will be changed." *(Blessed Mother – December 2, 1998)*

"Today, I advise you, whenever you are challenged in Holy Love, seek the Refuge of My Mother's Immaculate Heart. For it is flaws in Holy Love that result in lack of peace; even sin. My Mother, Who is always your Advocate, will take all your needs to My Heart in Heaven." *(Jesus – April 5, 2008)*

"Dear children, you are never in any situation alone, but always have recourse to the Refuge of Holy Love that is My Heart. My Heart is always united to the Heart of My Son. Every petition you place in My Heart is, therefore, passed into My Son's Most Sacred Heart. Our Hearts are united just as we desire every heart be united." *(Mary, Refuge of Holy Love – May 5, 2017)*

First, I (Maureen) saw the United Hearts; then Jesus came and He had the United Hearts in place of His Sacred Heart. He says: "My brothers and sisters, the peace of the world has been entrusted to My Mother's Immaculate Heart. My Mother's Heart is Holy Love. Therefore, be united in Holy Love and you will find peace." *(Jesus – September 25, 2015)*

Consecration to the United Hearts
"Most Worthy, United Hearts of Jesus and Mary, I willingly consecrate myself this day to You. I surrender to You all I own, both interior and exterior. Let my life be a continual hymn of praise to Your Most Holy United Hearts. Take the victories and defeats of this moment into Your Hearts. Use them, as You need them, to bring about Your Triumphant Reign. Amen."
(Blessed Mother – 1996)

UNITED HEARTS CHAPLET MEDITATIONS
11

(via foot path to St. Pio's Shrine)

"It is by means of this devotion the hardened heart can be made suppliant and touched by grace." *(The Eternal Father – November 11, 2002)*

"I have come to enlighten the world concerning the Revelation of the United Hearts. As still further has been stated, God's Love and His Mercy are one – always united. It is also true that the Cross and the Victory are one – never separate. This comes to life for you in the recitation of the *Chaplet of the United Hearts.* You pray in honor of the Sacred Heart of Jesus and the Immaculate Heart of Mary, Who in the end will triumph and reign. You then meditate on the Passion of Our Lord and the Sorrows of Mary. The last meditation is in Atonement to the Two Hearts. It is such atonement that will usher in the Triumph of the New Jerusalem." *(St. Thomas Aquinas – October 18, 2011)*

"The spirituality of the Chambers of Our United Hearts is great enough to pull the world back onto the path of righteousness. Therefore, along with the *Rosary of the Unborn*, propagate the little *Chaplet of the United Hearts* which will serve to lead many into the depths of these Chambers." *(Jesus – September 7, 2002)*

Promises for Praying The United Hearts Chaplet

1. "My Son promises He will answer all petitions surrendered to the United Hearts.
2. "Through the recitation of the Chaplet of the United Hearts, a more fervent reception of the Blessed Sacrament will be made [by those who are Catholic]."
3. "The United Hearts of Jesus and Mary are a fortress against evil."

(Our Lady – February 29, 1996)

UNITED HEARTS CHAPLET

NOTE: *The Chaplet is comprised of twenty (20) beads; five (5) sets each of one (1) Our Father and three (3) Hail Mary's. The following are the meditations given by Our Lady for each set.*

1. In Honor of the Sacred Heart of Jesus

I invite My children to realize the profound depth and perfection that comprises My Beloved Son's Heart. Allow yourselves to be drawn into this Vessel of perfect Love, Mercy, and Truth. Let the Flame of His Heart consume you and bring you to the heights of union with the Holy Trinity. To Him all honor and glory! Jesus, bestow on My children a hunger for salvation through devotion to Your Most Sacred Heart. *(Our Lady – February 7, 1998)*

>   *Our Father... Hail Mary... Hail Mary... Hail Mary...*

2. In Honor of the Immaculate Heart of Mary

Immaculate Heart of Mary, You are the purest vessel of grace, the definition of holiness, and a sign of the apocalypse. Mary, Your Heart is a Refuge of Holy Love – a countersign in an evil age. Dear Heart of Mary, it has been ordained that the conversion and peace of the world be entrusted to You. Only through Holy Love can the battle be won. As you, Heart of Mary, have been pierced by many swords, impale our hearts with the flaming arrow of Holy Love. Immaculate Heart of Mary, pray for us. *(Our Lady – March 7, 1998)*

>   *Our Father... Hail Mary... Hail Mary... Hail Mary...*

3. Meditating on the Passion of Our Lord

Jesus was willingly put to death for the sins of mankind. He died for each one and for all. From His Side flows, yet today, an unending font of Love and Mercy. Do not be reluctant, as Simon was reluctant, to embrace the crosses you are given. Many suffer the eternal flames of hell, for no one has been willing to suffer for them. Eternal Victim, truly present in the tabernacles of the world, pray for us. *(Our Lady – April 4, 1998)*

>   *Our Father... Hail Mary... Hail Mary... Hail Mary...*

4. Meditating on the Sorrows of Mary

As My Son suffered for you, I suffered as well, in My Intellect, in My Heart, and in My Body. My physical cross remained hidden. My emotional and intellectual crosses could only be guessed at – the intensity burning within Me. So too, should your suffering remain hidden, whenever possible, to gain merit for souls, grace for the world. *(Our Lady – May 2, 1998)*
    Our Father... Hail Mary... Hail Mary... Hail Mary...

5. In Atonement to the Hearts of Jesus and Mary

I invite you to understand that your 'yes' in the present moment to Holy Love is atoning to Our United Hearts. I tell you this, My little one, for to live in Holy Love in every moment requires heroic self-discipline and surrender to God's Divine Will through Holy Love. You can sacrifice many great things – possessions, events, and more – but none so great as your own will. This is the greatest atonement. *(Our Lady – June 6, 1998)*
    Our Father... Hail Mary... Hail Mary... Hail Mary...

*(At the end of the Chaplet prayers,
on the medal, say the following Prayer
to the United Hearts of Jesus and Mary.)*

Prayer to the United Hearts of Jesus and Mary

O United Hearts of Jesus and Mary, You are All-Grace, All-Mercy, All-Love. Let my heart be joined to Yours, so that my every need is present in Your United Hearts. Most especially, shed Your Grace upon this particular need:

(State Need)

Help me to recognize and accept Your loving Will in my life. Amen. *(Jesus – February 10, 1996)*

Holy and Sacred Wounds of the United Hearts
of Jesus and Mary answer my prayer.
(Jesus – March 26, 1996)

Section 3. Journey of Holiness

ST. PIO OF PIETRELCINA SHRINE 12

('Padre Pio')
Patron of Holy Love Ministries

St. Pio has promised to give his Priestly Blessing to those who ask his intercession at his shrine.

"Sometimes, desperation provides the groundwork for great miracles. Always, faith is the backbone of any miracle. Unless the miracle is believed, it can be explained away, discounted or never occur at all. Many of God's miracles are never believed in, and so the grace goes unattended."

"It is so here, even at this site. Some will never believe. They receive nothing. Others believe a little; so (he shrugs his shoulders) they receive a little. Some receive acceptance of the Father's Will – a great grace. Some who have desperate needs are granted them." *(St. Pio of Pietrelcina – July 15, 2012)*

"Both of these (St. Thérèse and Padre Pio) were victims of love – Holy Love. Both made great strides to bridge the span between Heaven and earth through Holy Love. The good Father Pio carried visible signs on his body of this love, a love he shared with His Savior." *(Mary, Refuge of Holy Love – June 18, 1997)*

Surrender of Heart to Victimhood of Love

"Dear Sacred Heart of Jesus and Sorrowing Heart of Mary, I give You my whole heart, every joy and sorrow, every iniquity and all merit that You find in it today. I offer to You my desire to be Your victim of love. With this desire, see my trust in Your Will for me, and allow this trust to console You. Amen."
(Jesus – April 18, 2003 / Good Friday 3:00 p.m.)

STATIONS OF THE CROSS

"I stand at the entrance of the Stations of the Cross blessing all." *(St. Pio of Pietrelcina – September 23, 2013)*

"Those who recite the Stations will find solace and healing. Much peace will be given in the Station area. I will accompany those who pray the Way of the Cross there." *(Our Lady – November 12, 1997)*

"There is a special angel assigned to each Station of the Cross and at each statue whose duty is to inspire deeper devotion in the hearts of passersby." *(Mary of the Holy Angels – August 2, 2009)*

"Jesus says that those souls who come on pilgrimage to the property, and prayerfully visit the Shrine of My Sorrows or the Stations of the Cross, and also pray the *Consecration of the Heart of the World to Our United Hearts*, will receive the *Complete Blessing of Our United Hearts*." (Blessed Mother – May 16, 2012)

(See page 40 for the Consecration prayer. See page 81 for the Promises attendant to the United Hearts Blessing.)

STATIONS OF THE CROSS

"After each Station, simply say:"

"Jesus, meek and humble of Heart, make my heart like unto Thine."

Section 3. Journey of Holiness   59

1. JESUS IS CONDEMNED TO DEATH
Lesson
"The First Station commemorates My condemnation to death. I suffered for all who are condemned falsely and all who are unrepentant."
Meditation
"Jesus, many who witnessed Your miracles agreed on Your death sentence. Have mercy on those who witness the miracles at this site but still refuse to believe."

"Jesus, meek and humble of Heart..."

2. JESUS CARRIES HIS CROSS
Lesson
"The Second Station represents My acceptance of My Cross. How many refuse despite all their sins to carry their cross."
Meditation
"You accepted this Cross out of love for Your Father's Divine Will and love of me. Help me to accept the crosses I am given for love of You."

"Jesus, meek and humble of Heart..."

3. JESUS FALLS THE FIRST TIME
Lesson
"The Third Station is My first fall. So many slip into sin and become discouraged by one fall."
Meditation
"Jesus, I offer to the Father this first fall. I ask the Father to help me never to fall into mortal sin."

"Jesus, meek and humble of Heart..."

4. JESUS MEETS HIS MOTHER
Lesson
"The Fourth Station commemorates My encounter with My Mother. How often souls have the opportunity to console those in need but never do it."

Meditation

"Jesus, I join you now in this present moment in consoling the Sorrowful Heart of Your Mother."
"Jesus, meek and humble of Heart..."

5. SIMON UNWILLINGLY HELPS JESUS CARRY HIS CROSS

Lesson

"The Fifth Station represents Simon's reluctance to assist Me. So many souls desire to be close to Me but try to do so without carrying their cross."

Meditation

"Jesus, help me to accept the crosses You send with love. Help me always to be a willing instrument in Your Hands."
"Jesus, meek and humble of Heart..."

6. VERONICA WIPES THE FACE OF JESUS

Lesson

"The Sixth Station remembers Veronica wiping My Face. Think how she had to die to herself, setting aside her own safety and welfare in order to comfort Me. Be self-effacing."

Meditation

"Through love of You, help me to wipe out all my sinful inclinations, Jesus."
"Jesus, meek and humble of Heart..."

7. JESUS FALLS THE SECOND TIME

Lesson

"This Station represents another fall. Do not fall into sinful habits."

Meditation

"Jesus, do not let me repeat my sins. Keep me from falling."
"Jesus, meek and humble of Heart..."

Section 3. Journey of Holiness   61

8. JESUS CONSOLES THE WOMEN IN JERUSALEM
Lesson
"The Eighth Station remembers My consoling the women of Jerusalem. Allow Me to be your consolation when others fail you."
Meditation
"Console me, Jesus, so that I do not become discouraged by my sinful inclinations."
"Jesus, meek and humble of Heart..."

9. JESUS FALLS A THIRD TIME
Lesson
"The Ninth Station recalls another fall. Search your hearts and overcome recurrent sinful patterns."
Meditation
"Jesus, help me to rise above my sins, and to pursue personal holiness."
"Jesus, meek and humble of Heart..."

10. JESUS IS STRIPPED OF HIS GARMENTS
Lesson
"The Tenth Station recalls how I was stripped of My Garments. Strip your hearts of all vanity."
Meditation
"Jesus, strip me of all that stands between us."
"Jesus, meek and humble of Heart...

11. JESUS IS NAILED TO THE CROSS
Lesson
"The Eleventh Station recalls how I was nailed to the cross. It was My Father's Will that held Me to the cross though the nails pierced My Flesh. Be devoted to the Will of My Father."
Meditation
"Jesus, the nails pierced Your Flesh just as my sins pierced Your Heart. Forgive me."
"Jesus, meek and humble of Heart..."

12. JESUS DIES ON THE CROSS
Lesson
"The Twelfth Station commemorates My Death. Do not worship this life which is passing. Let your hearts ascend to Heaven."
Meditation
"You stayed on the Cross until death, dear Jesus. It was not the nails that held you there but love of Your Father's Will. Help me to love God's Will for me—no matter the cost."

"Jesus, meek and humble of Heart..."

13. JESUS IS TAKEN DOWN FROM THE CROSS
Lesson
"The Thirteenth Station sees Me taken down from the cross. This death of Mine was a victory in disguise. How many do not see the disguises Satan wears?"
Meditation
"Jesus, Your Sorrowful Mother held You in Her Arms. I ask Your Sorrowing Mother now to forgive me for any sins I committed that You died for. I ask Mary to present my contrite heart to Her Son."

"Jesus, meek and humble of Heart..."

14. JESUS IS LAID IN THE SEPULCHRE
Lesson
"The Fourteenth Station – I am laid to rest in the sepulchre. Do not rest in doing good and opposing evil until it is time for your eternal rest. So many waste precious moments given to them to earn their salvation."
Meditation
"Lovingly, Your Mother prepared Your Broken Body for the tomb, Jesus. Ask Your Mother to lovingly prepare my heart torn by sin, to receive You in Holy Communion."

"Jesus, meek and humble of Heart...
(Jesus – March 7, 2011 and March 24, 2016)

Section 3. Journey of Holiness 63

 ST. JOSEPH SHRINE AND LAKE

"The fathers who go to my shrine in the United Hearts Field will be anointed with Wisdom and Prudence in order to better govern their families. Each family member has a responsibility towards personal holiness. If they answer this call, they will find peace and unity within the family unit." *(St. Joseph – June 1, 2014)*

"Today I tell you, those who make pilgrimage to St. Joseph's Shrine in the United Hearts Field will be inspired towards family unity. This grace, while not overpowering free will, will be the inspiration some need towards forgiveness." *(Jesus – June 1, 2014)*

Prayer for St. Joseph's Protection
"Good St. Joseph – Defender of the Truth and Terror of Demons – I place all members of my family under your gaze. Protect them and guide them along their way to salvation. Amen."
(St. Joseph – May 1, 2016)

SPECIAL GRACES AND BLESSINGS RECEIVED WHILE MAKING THE JOURNEY OF HOLINESS

Heaven bestows many graces and blessings on pilgrims as they make the Journey of Holiness, including:

1. **As you enter and walk the property**

   - Jesus' Sacred Heart greets and surrounds you.
   - You receive Jesus' Anointing of Divine Love.
   - You are plunged into the First Chamber of the United Hearts as Jesus places the Seal of Discernment on your forehead, if your heart is sincere.
   - You receive the Blessing of Truth from Jesus, if your heart is sincere.
   - You receive Our Lady's Special Blessing, if your heart is open and receptive to the Messages and graces offered here.
   - You receive an illumination of conscience as St. Michael's Sword pricks your heart, if you come in humility, not arrogance.
   - You receive God the Father's Blessing of Paternal Love, if your heart is open and accepts the Messages of Holy and Divine Love.
   - Jesus, Blessed Mother, many saints and angels accompany you.
   - You feel Heaven's peace.
   - Priests receive an extra angel to guard their vocations and move more rapidly through the Chambers of the United Hearts.

   "If you visit this prayer site with open hearts, the angels who are My messengers, will give you a fresh perspective as to your state of life and your problems. You will be more prepared to see things as I do. Sometimes solutions are at your fingertips. Other times you will receive the grace you need to follow the path I am calling you upon. The grace will be given to you to bear your crosses." *(God the Father – July 8, 2021)*

Section 3. Journey of Holiness 65

2. **The Sorrowful Mother Shrine and Lake of Tears**

   - You receive the Complete Blessing of the United Hearts, if you pray the 'Consecration of the Heart of the World to the United Hearts'.
   - Our Lady alleviates the afflicted, makes steadfast the wavering heart, and consoles the downtrodden.
   - The Lake of Tears water brings special consolation to the mothers who sorrow for their wayward children.
   - Our Lady unites your heart to Her own Sorrowful and Immaculate Heart.
   - Many angels in attendance carry petitions to Heaven as Our Lady desires; Our Lady responds to them according to God's Will.

3. **The Arbor**

   - Our Lady looks down on you and blesses you.

4. **The Lake of the Holy Angels**

   - Our Lady reigns over the lake and an angel from each choir stands in attendance.
   - Many graces are given, faith is protected and Satan's snares are revealed to souls.

5. **God the Father Shrine**

   - You receive God the Father's Blessing of Paternal Joy, if your heart is open.

6. **St. Michael Shrine and Lake**

   - St. Michael extends his Shield of Truth to you.
   - You find a respite of prayer for rebellious souls.
   - Parents of wayward children find peace.
   - Priests will return to the true Tradition of Faith.
   - The lake holds special blessings for the Remnant Faithful.

7. **The Field of the United Hearts**

   - You receive Our Lady's Blessing of Holy Love.

8. Maranatha Spring

- The Lourdes of this continent and hemisphere, with comparable healing graces for both body and soul.
- Reveals Truths, heals, and brings peace.
- Numerous souls find conversion.
- The miraculous healing waters wash you clean.
- You are immediately surrounded by a myriad of angels when you bless yourself with the water.
- You are assigned an additional guardian angel who tries to bring the peace of Holy Love into your soul and inspires the Message of Holy Love to come alive in your heart.
- Your conscience is laid bare.
- The water and objects carried away from this site will carry the spirit of peace.
- Carry the water with you as protection.

9. St. Pio of Pietrelcina Shrine

- You receive St. Pio's priestly blessing if you ask his intercession at his shrine.

10. The Stations of the Cross

- St. Pio blesses you as you enter the Stations.
- Our Lady accompanies you as you pray the Way of the Cross.
- You receive the Complete Blessing of the United Hearts if you pray the 'Consecration of the Heart of the World to the United Hearts'.

11. St. Joseph Shrine and Lake

- Fathers are anointed with Wisdom and Prudence.
- Family members are inspired towards family unity.

Note: The water from Maranatha Spring and the various lakes will change many hearts and heal many of physical difficulties.

Section 4. Aquinas Center

ST. THOMAS AQUINAS LEARNING CENTER

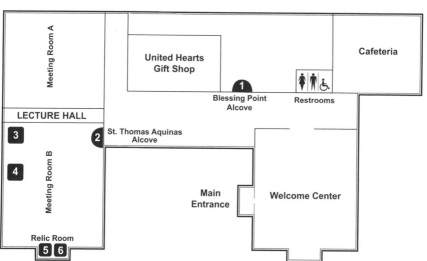

WELCOME CENTER

- Ministry Offices
- Pilgrim Orientations
- Video Tours

- Pilgrim Photos
- Pilgrim Testimonies
- Information Kiosk

CAFETERIA
- Vending Machines
- Special Event Catering
- Veranda with Picnic Area

UNITED HEARTS GIFT SHOP
(Open Daily)
- Books and Gifts
- Religious Articles
- Rosary of the Unborn
- Chaplet of the Unborn

Meeting Room A

LECTURE HALL
- St. Thomas Aquinas
- Our Lady of Grace
- Missionary Image of Our Lady of Guadalupe
- Relic of Our Lady's Hair
- Our Lady of Fatima

Meeting Room B

Section 4. Aquinas Center

1. OUR LADY'S BLESSING POINT

(Located in the alcove next to the United Hearts Gift Shop.)

(Write your prayer requests on a piece of paper, touch them to the Blessing Point, and place them in the basket. Then venerate this spot by kissing the glass.)

> Throughout the early 1990's, Our Lady appeared to the Visionary during prayer services held at Seven Hills, Ohio. Our Lady hovered over one particular area of the room at the prayer meetings. No matter where Maureen would sit, Our Lady always appeared in the same place. Eventually, this area of the carpeting over which Our Lady appeared began to radiate the fragrance of roses. Our Lady advised the Ministry to mark off this area with a circle (representing eternity), and to place rosaries and other holy items there for special blessings.
>
> When the Ministry moved from the Seven Hills site, Our Lady directed the Ministry to cut out the carpeted area where "HEAVEN AND EARTH HAVE MET" so the blessings could continue for those who venerate this special area of grace.

"Encourage My children to come to My Blessing Point, for it is here I will open My Heart to humanity." *(Our Lady – March 8, 1993)*

"Dear children, I leave you this sign of My Presence amongst you. Press your rosaries and other objects to it. Kiss it and venerate it. THIS IS WHERE HEAVEN AND EARTH HAVE MET. I promise many, many graces to those who do so." *(Our Lady – March 22, 1992)*

"Each will receive a grace particular to his or her own needs. God knows best what to give." *(Our Lady – March 23, 1992)*

"The graces given at My Mother's Blessing Point let faults rise to the surface so that the soul is awakened and prodded into dealing with them." *(Jesus – August 1, 1992)*

"Any article you place here will carry with it special grace to heal the infirm, to comfort and convert hearts, and to take power over darkness." *(Our Lady – August 5, 1992)*

"Please make it known My Presence is continually and always at Maranatha Spring and at the Blessing Point. For here I intend to grant many favors." *(Our Lady – May 23, 1994)*

"This (apparition site) is the place where Heaven has touched earth. The Blessing Point is a special sign of this grace. Come and see." *(Mary, Refuge of Holy Love – March 13, 2016)*

"I welcome all who have answered My call to come here. I am waiting to take each petition to the Heart of My Son." *(Our Lady – July 30, 1992)*

The Memorare

Remember, O most gracious Virgin Mary, that never was it known that anyone who fled to Thy protection, implored Thy help, or sought Thine intercession was left unaided.

Inspired by this confidence, I fly unto Thee, O Virgin of virgins, my mother; to Thee do I come, before Thee I stand, sinful and sorrowful. O Mother of the Word Incarnate, despise not my petitions, but in Thy mercy hear and answer me.

Amen.

Section 4. Aquinas Center	71

2   ST. THOMAS AQUINAS

"Holy Love is the doorway to grace. It is a reflection of God's Love – a mirror image of Divine Love. The way to achieve the fulfillment of all your petitions, then, is to perfect your heart in Holy Love." *(St. Thomas Aquinas – January 13, 2010)*

> **Consecration to Holy Love in the Present Moment**
>
> *"Heavenly Father, I consecrate my heart in this present moment to Holy Love. Keep me mindful of this throughout the day so that all my thoughts and actions will proceed from Holy Love."*
>
> *"I cover this petition with the Most Precious Blood of Jesus, your Son, and surround it with the Tears of His Most Sorrowful Mother. Amen."*
>
> *(St. Thomas Aquinas – January 21, 2002)*

3   OUR LADY OF GRACE

"Grace is the Will of God in action. Often, as a modest lady, grace remains hidden in the background. Sometimes this 'Lady Grace' is coaxed out into the open so that all can admire and enjoy her."

"Such is the case here in this Mission and at this apparition site. Miracle after miracle occurs here and will continue to do so. God is coaxing souls in the spirituality of Holy Love. Look to the skies. Look to the healings at the Spring and by the lakes. Come and revere My Son's Passion in the Stations. Come and console Me in My Sorrows. I promise to be there listening."

"Many graces are awaiting those who will come with faith – many graces that you do not even expect and can't even imagine." *(Blessed Mother – July 11, 2010)*

"I will step out of the statue as a sign of My greeting those who come. This too will be photographed." *(Our Lady – November 12, 1997)*

> **Morning Prayer of Thanksgiving for Daily Graces**
> *"Eternal Father*, I thank You now for all the graces You will send me through the Immaculate Heart of Mary. Open my heart to recognize and to respond to each grace. Amen."
> *(Our Lady of Grace – May 8, 2015 / Feast of Our Lady of Grace)*

4. MISSIONARY IMAGE OF OUR LADY OF GUADALUPE

Once again Our Lady comes as Our Lady of Guadalupe and changes into Mary, Refuge of Holy Love. "I show Myself to you in this way, My daughter, to help you to understand the connection between these Apparitions. Just as My Image at Guadalupe was in support of life in the womb, I am once again the New Eve as Refuge of Holy Love, protecting and offering shelter to all life and bringing Jesus to you in the heart of these Messages." *(December 12, 2008 – Feast of Our Lady of Guadalupe)*

> **Prayer to Recognize Life at Conception**
> *"Dear Jesus*, just as Your Mother carried You in Her Virginal Womb in Holy Love, move the conscience of the world to accept the Truth that all human life begins at the moment of conception. Help the world to see that this is God's Divine Will which is Holy Love. Amen."
> *(Our Lady of Guadalupe – December 12, 2010)*

Section 4. Aquinas Center 73

RELIC – A STRAND OF BLESSED MOTHER'S HAIR
5

The glass-covered reliquary contains a Strand of Blessed Mother's Hair given to the Visionary on September 15, 1997.

"It is by such a frail thread that the world hangs suspended over the abyss – the abyss between Heaven and earth. This is why, My daughter, I give you the Strand of My Hair to venerate; and, as you do so, to see the frail position earth has placed herself in. Only with much love, prayer, and sacrifice will the frail strand remain." *(Our Lady – June 4, 1998)*

> **Prayer of Petition to Live in the Divine Will**
> *"Heavenly Father, during this time of world crisis, let all souls find their peace and security in Your Divine Will. Give each soul the grace to understand that Your Will is Holy Love in the present moment."*
> *"Benevolent Father, illuminate each conscience to see the ways that he is not living in Your Will. Grant the world the grace to change and the time in which to do it. Amen."*
> *(Mary, Mother of God – September 28, 2001)*

OUR LADY OF FATIMA
6

"Holy Love is the ongoing present-day Fatima." *(Blessed Mother – October 13, 2011)*

"At Fatima, my dear sister, the peace of the world was entrusted to the Immaculate Heart of My Mother. But in these Revelations given to the world at this site, the soul of the world is given the key with which to enter Her Heart and to be at peace." *(Jesus – October 13, 2001)*

"My efforts here are the same as they were at Fatima – to save souls and to bring peace to the world ... My peace plan from Heaven is this." She holds out the Rosary of the Unborn. *(See Appendix A.)* *(Our Lady of Fatima – May 13, 2016)*

Prayer for Unity and Peace
Amongst All People and All Nations
"Heavenly Father, we come to Your Paternal Heart seeking peace amongst all people and all nations. Bring into harmony with Your Divine Will all human life, all of nature – even the cosmos itself."

"Protect all of creation from Satan's destructive plans. We know that war must be in hearts before it is in the world. Inspire all mankind, dear Father, to choose love of God and neighbor, which leads to true peace, for we know this is Your Will for us. Amen."
(St. Thomas Aquinas – July 23, 2006)

Section 5.
United Hearts Chapel

UNITED HEARTS CHAPEL

1 ST. JUDE THADDEUS, APOSTLE

***Patron Saint of Lost Causes
and Desperate Cases***

"There are many factors that make up courage. The soul must be deep in faith, hope and love, for these three beget trust. Trust bears the fruit of courage. It is a courageous heart that can persevere despite all odds." *(St. Jude – October 28, 2002)*

> **Prayer for the Gift of Fortitude**
> *"Lord,* send forth Your Spirit and ask Him to place the gift of fortitude in my heart. Through this grace of fortitude, help me to be patient in the face of all trials and difficulties. Give me the courage through fortitude to press on amidst every difficulty. Amen."
> *(Jesus – May 14, 2010)*

2 JESUS CRUCIFIED

"Today, the world holds the Cross in low esteem. Sacrificial suffering is rarely upheld from the pulpit. My Corpus upon the Cross has become unpopular. For the most part, the role of My Redemption for all mankind takes a back seat to disordered self-love."

"Yet, the value of My Cross has not diminished and never will be. Your devotion to My Cross is My Glory in the world. This love of My efforts – My Passion and Death – garners you many favors. Your invocation to My Precious Blood spells Satan's defeat. Never become immune to the Power of the Cross. Kiss My Wounds with your little sacrifices. Together, we can change hearts. Together, My Cross will be exalted." *(Jesus – September 14, 2013)*

"As I underwent my Passion and Death, I saw this Mission take form and it was a great consolation." *(Jesus – February 17, 2000)*

Section 5. United Hearts Chapel

> **Consecration to the Cross**
>
> *"My Jesus,* I consecrate myself this day to Your Holy Cross. Just as You took upon Yourself that great Cross for the sake of all humanity, so I vow to embrace the crosses in my life. Everything I suffer I give back to You, my Sweet Jesus, to atone for my sins and those of all the world. I will begin and end each day at the foot of Your Cross, together with our most Blessed Mother and Saint John, our brother. My only pleasure will be to comfort You, my Sweet Savior. Amen."
>
> *(Blessed Virgin Mary – December 4, 1990)*

3. ST. JOHN VIANNEY
The Curé D'Ars and Patron Saint of Priests

"Reserve a side chapel to the good and Blessed John Marie Vianney ... It is so I can call priests back to the true Faith, to Tradition and away from much compromise. When My priests come, as they will, I will be present, praying with them." *(Our Lady – May 30, 1995)*

"I have come to tell each one of you that anything you do without love in your heart is wasted. Priests in particular must pray for love of prayer, sacrifice and penance, for this is the way of conversion for their flock that they have been entrusted with. Do not hesitate to ask me to intercede for you, whether you are a priest or lay person. This is a special grace to love penance, prayer and sacrifice. I will help you with it." *(St. John Vianney – July 14, 2006)*

"Each time before you begin to pray, recall in your heart how much God the Father loves you, that He gave His Only Begotten Son to be given up to death for you. Then recall how much Jesus loves you, that He surrendered everything on your behalf. Always return love to Him Who is All-Love. (The Curé motions toward the Crucifix.) Priests should remind their flocks of these Truths before they begin to pray." *(St. John Vianney – October 9, 2009)*

> **The Laity's Prayer for Holy Priests**
> *"Dear Jesus,* place all vocations and every priest in Your Most Sacred Heart. We pray:"
> - "All priests value their vocation and pursue personal holiness by living in Holy Love and going deeper into the virtues."
> - "Please strengthen the Tradition of Faith in all priests."
> - "Protect Your priests from all scandal and exploitation."
> - "Help Your priests to know their first obligation is to minister the Sacraments to the laity."
> - "Strip Your priests of attachments to the world – all concerns for power, money, popularity or corporal desires – just as You, Jesus, were stripped at the Tenth Station of the Cross."
> - "Bring all priests into the Divine Will of Your Father. Amen."
> *(St. John Vianney – January 19, 2013)*

4 ST. THÉRÈSE OF LISIEUX

Patroness of Holy Love Ministries
and
Patron Saint of Missionaries

"My brothers and sisters, take as your example this little saint who rose to be a Doctor of the Church. She did so by offering everything – even the smallest, smallest thing – with great love to My Sacred Heart, making it acceptable and worthy of converting a sinner." *(Jesus – October 1, 2010)*

"Every present moment holds a bounty of sacrifices to be

Section 5. United Hearts Chapel

offered to God. These little sacrifices combine to become great graces for the soul and for humanity in general. Ask me and I will help you to discover these small sacrifices. Offer them with love." *(St. Thérèse of Lisieux – October 1, 2015)*

"God did not create each soul only for his own salvation, but also for the salvation of those whose lives they touch. It is through the example of a virtuous life souls are attracted to holiness and salvation. The steps each soul takes towards his own perfection in Holy Love should be a sweetness that attracts other souls. Each soul then becomes a missionary in his own way, propagating and encouraging Holy Love wherever possible." *(St. Thérèse of Lisieux – January 5, 2016)*

> **Missionary Prayer of Holy Love**
> *"Immaculate Mary, Virgin and Queen of Heaven and Earth*, consume my soul in the Flame of Holy Love that is Your Heart. Help me to be Your Love in the world and to hasten Your victorious reign through My prayers and acts of Holy Love. Spread Your Mantle of Protection over Holy Love Ministries. Lead us and guide us. Intercede on our behalf before the throne of Jesus, Your Son. Amen."
> *(Our Lady – September 21, 1994)*

5. ST. JOSEPH AND THE CHILD JESUS

"God so deems that I be recognized as *'Foster Father of All Humanity'*. As such, I must call all of mankind into the Chambers of the United Hearts. This spiritual journey places the soul securely upon the path of salvation – even sanctification. It is in traveling this path that my foster children will discover their peace and security." *(St. Joseph – March 19, 2011)*

"When invoked by this title, he is protector of life from the moment of conception." *(Blessed Mother – December 16, 2010)*

> **Prayer to End Abortion**
> *"O Divine Infant Jesus,* present in the womb of Mary at conception by the power of the Holy Spirit, present in the crib at Bethlehem in obedience to the Will of God, open the heart of mankind to see that true peace will only come when there is peace in the womb. Awaken mankind and help each soul to surrender to the Will of his Divine Creator. Amen."
> *(Angel Alanus – October 7, 2010)*

"Please understand that it is important for individuals to be consecrated to the United Hearts, but even more important is that whole families be thus consecrated. For it is in this consecration to the United Hearts that families will live and breathe, act and speak according to God's Holy and Divine Will." *(St. Joseph – June 5, 2011)*

*(See Appendix B for the '**Family Consecration to the United Hearts**' given by St. Thomas Aquinas.)*

"Families entrusted to my care receive my Fatherly Protection against the evils of the day. I will warn their hearts of potential threats of evil, as I am the Terror of Demons." *(St. Joseph – May 1, 2016)*

IMAGE OF THE UNITED HEARTS OF THE MOST HOLY TRINITY AND IMMACULATE MARY

(See explanation on pages 12–14.)

"Heaven is very pleased with the (United Hearts) Image above the altar. Tonight I ask that you rededicate yourselves to spreading the Consecration of the Heart of the World to Our United Hearts." *(Jesus – March 7, 2014)*

(See page 40 to pray the 'Consecration of the Heart of the World to the United Hearts.')

Section 5. United Hearts Chapel   81

"When you arise in the morning, surrender your hearts to Our United Hearts wherein you will be protected and safeguarded against evil; then I will extend to you the Blessing of Our United Hearts, and you will be at peace." *(Jesus – October 31, 2011)*

The Complete Blessing of the United Hearts is transferrable to others, so please pass it on by thinking, speaking or writing:

"I extend to you (or insert name)
the Complete Blessing of the United Hearts."

Promises with Respect to the United Hearts Blessing

1. It will gratify the most distant hearts and bring them closer to Jesus.
2. It will strengthen spiritually and often physically.
3. It is preparing mankind for Jesus' Second Coming.
4. It carries with it special graces of healing – both spiritual and physical.
5. It will be a deterrent to Satan and will bring with it disclosure of evil in hearts and in the world.
6. It will draw everyone who receives it to a devotion to the United Hearts.
7. It inspires souls to come closer to the Paternal Love of the Father.
8. It hastens Jesus' victory in hearts.
9. Through it, trust comes more easily into the heart.

It is important to note that the Complete Blessing of the United Hearts carries with it the combined graces of all of the Blessings given to this Mission, including:

10. It enables one to live in the virtue of Holy Love.
11. It is a strength in adversity, patience amidst trial.
12. It brings with it the grace of zeal for holiness.
13. It extends over the soul and in the soul abundant graces to choose the Divine Will in every present moment.
14. It gives peace.
15. It assists the soul in carrying his cross.

7 MARY, REFUGE OF HOLY LOVE

"(This Image of Mary, Refuge of Holy Love) carries with it very many special graces which the world needs today. *(See pages 10–12)*. Those who venerate this Image, either in picture or three-dimensional form, will be drawn into deeper personal holiness. Their thoughts, words and deeds will be clarified in Holy Love." *(Blessed Mother – January 19, 2010)*

Consecration to the Flame of Holy Love

"Immaculate Heart of Mary, humbly, I ask that You take my heart into the Flame of Holy Love, that is the Spiritual Refuge of all mankind. Do not look upon my faults and failings, but allow these iniquities to be burned away by this purifying Flame."

"Through Holy Love, help me to be sanctified in the present moment, and in so doing, give to You, dear Mother, my every thought, word, and action. Take me and use me according to Your great pleasure. Allow me to be Your instrument in the world, all for the greater glory of God and towards Your victorious reign. Amen."
(Blessed Mother – April 16, 1995)

8 SACRED HEART OF JESUS

(This statue has been seen to weep.)

"Do you know why I cry? How many times have I sent My Mother to this site? I weep for those who do not come, do not pray, will not listen, and will not believe. Greater still is the pain I feel by those who blaspheme the visitations of My Mother. And the Message – so pure – so clear – resonating My Gospels, how can it be controversial? Yes, we must pray. I will continue to weep until the triumph. With a passionate Heart I will continue to weep." *(Jesus – May 27, 1998)*

Section 5. United Hearts Chapel   83

"My Sacred Heart greets and surrounds every soul that comes onto the property, whether it is for the first time or the three hundredth time. I am always here; My Heart is always exposed over the property. I long to inflame the hearts of those who come here with Divine Love." *(Jesus – June 14, 2012)*

Consecration to Divine Love

"My Jesus, Divine Love Itself, I consecrate myself completely to You. In and through this consecration I unite my soul to Divine Love, understanding that in so doing I will be a martyr of love. I choose to seek only Your good pleasure in the present moment, Jesus. Thus, I surrender to You my health, my appearance, and even my own comforts. Through this surrender I pray that Divine Love will be victorious in every heart. Enfolded within this consecration to Your Divine Love, sweet Jesus, find my 'yes' to the Divine Will of God in every moment and with every breath."

"I seek nothing that You would not have me seek. I love no person, place, or thing beyond Your Will for Me. I embrace every cross You permit and cherish every grace You provide. Amen."

(Jesus – October 12, 1999)

Request for Assistance to Live the Consecration to Divine Love

"Heavenly Father, Lord Jesus Christ, and Holy Spirit of God, I come before You as I have consecrated my body and soul to Divine Love. I ask Your assistance in living out this consecration in every present moment. Help me to surrender to every cross, and to recognize and respond to every precious grace You place in my life. Through my consecration to Divine Love, I beg Your assistance in annihilating my own will and living in Your Divine Will. Amen."

(Jesus – October 14, 1999)

Jesus is here and He is holding His Sacred Heart in His Hand. He now holds it forward and says: "Brothers and sisters, I offer you the confines of My Most Sacred Heart, which these days has turned Mournful, due to the abuse of authority and compromise of Truth. My Heart is the perfection of Divine Love." *(Jesus – June 12, 2015 / Solemnity of the Most Sacred Heart of Jesus)*

Discernment of Truth between Good and Evil

"*Most Mournful Heart of Jesus*, assist me in discerning good from evil. Help me to recognize the abuse of authority and the compromise of Truth. In this way, be my protection. Amen."

(Our Lady – November 23, 2015)

Mournful Heart of Jesus

9 ST. MARTIN DE PORRES

Patron Saint of Social Justice, Racial Harmony and Mixed-Race People

"When I was in the world I made myself accountable for every scrap of food, every remnant of clothing, every coin that I was made charge of and, of course, every present moment. What my community could not use was freely given to the poor. None of my sacrifices were unwarranted. If this was so in my day, how much more is it so today?" *(St. Martin de Porres – July 21, 2004)*

Consecration to Self-Denial

"*Dear Jesus, Divine and Beloved Savior,* today I surrender to You every pain – physical, spiritual or emotional. I will not complain about inconveniences, demands upon my time, breaches of privacy or the rudeness of those You put in my life today. With Your help, I will accept each present moment with Holy Love. Amen."

(St. Martin de Porres – November 3, 2006)

APPENDIX A

Our Lady Gives the World
THE ROSARY OF THE UNBORN™ *and* THE CHAPLET OF THE UNBORN
To End Abortion

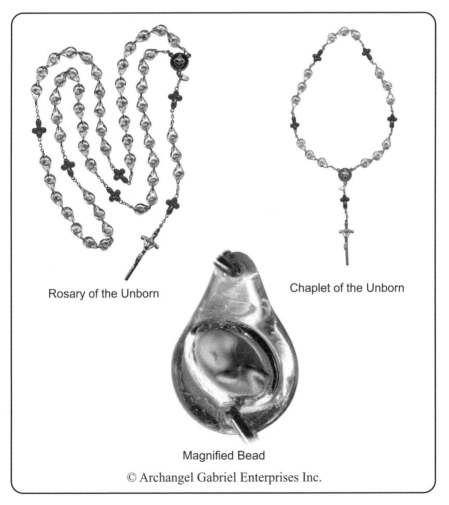

Rosary of the Unborn

Chaplet of the Unborn

Magnified Bead

© Archangel Gabriel Enterprises Inc.

www.RosaryoftheUnborn.com

VISION OF THE ROSARY OF THE UNBORN

Our Lady comes in white. In front of Her and suspended in the air is an unusual rosary. The Our Father beads are droplets of blood in the shape of a cross. The Hail Mary beads are light blue teardrops with unborn babies inside of them. The cross is gleaming gold. Our Lady says: "I come in praise of Jesus, My Son. I come as Prophetess of these times."

"The rosary you see is Heaven's way of describing to you the weapon that will overcome this evil of abortion. Heaven weeps for the cost of this great sin. The history and the future of all nations has been changed because of this atrocity against God's gift of life."

"Today, sadly, much responsibility must be placed on the laity who are consecrated to Me. I cannot depend on Church leadership to unite in an effort to vanquish the enemy through the Rosary. Even My Apparitions have caused division by Satan's efforts to thwart My plans."

"So today, on My feast day, I am calling all My children to unite in My Heart. Do not allow pride to divide you according to which Apparition you will follow. Become part of the Flame of My Heart. Be united in love and in the prayer weapon of My Rosary. The evil of abortion can be conquered by your efforts and through My Grace."

"Propagate the image I have shown you today."

(October 7, 1997 – Feast of the Holy Rosary)

Promises for Praying the Rosary of the Unborn

1. "Praise be to Jesus. I see you are using the new Rosary of the Unborn. I affirm to you, My daughter, that **each *'Hail Mary'* prayed from a loving heart will rescue one of these innocent lives from death by abortion.** When you use this rosary, call to mind My Sorrowful Immaculate Heart which continually sees the sin of abortion played out in every present moment. I give to you this special sacramental* with which to heal My Motherly Heart."

    Maureen asks: "Blessed Mother, do you mean any *'Hail Mary'* or just one prayed on the Rosary of the Unborn?"

    Blessed Mother: "This is a special grace attached to this particular rosary. It should always be used to pray against abortion. You will please make this known."

    (Our Lady as the Sorrowful Mother – July 2, 2001)

> ***Note:*** *Catholics believe that, in order to be a sacramental, the rosary must be blessed by a Catholic Priest.*

Appendix A 87

2. "Please tell the world that each *'Our Father'* recited on the Rosary of the Unborn assuages My grieving Heart. Further, it withholds the Arm of Justice." *(Jesus – August 3, 2001)*

3. "The greatest promise I give you in regards to this rosary is this: **Every Rosary prayed from the heart to its completion on these beads mitigates the punishment as yet withstanding for the sin of abortion** ... When I say the punishment as yet withstanding for the sin of abortion, I mean the punishment each soul deserves for taking part in this sin. Then too, I also refer to the greater punishment that awaits the world for embracing this sin." *(Jesus – August 3, 2001)*

4. "If a group is gathered who are praying for the unborn from the heart and only one person has in their possession the Rosary of the Unborn, **I will honor each *'Hail Mary'* from each person in the group** as if they were holding the Rosary of the Unborn themselves." *(Jesus – February 28, 2005)*

VISION OF THE CHAPLET OF THE UNBORN

Blessed Mother says: "I have come with yet another important weapon in the fight against abortion. As you know, abortion is the one crime which, if conquered, would change the future of the world. The weapon I now hand off to you is the Chaplet of the Unborn."

Blessed Mother holds out a chaplet with five sets of three Hail Marys and one Our Father – like the Chaplet of the United Hearts. The beads are like the beads on the Rosary of the Unborn. *(March 24, 2013)*

Promises for Praying the Chaplet of the Unborn

1. "Every time the Chaplet is prayed from the heart, some soul contemplating abortion will have a change of heart."

2. "Each time the Chaplet is prayed from the heart, some soul will be reconciled with the Truth of what abortion really is – the taking of a life."

3. "The Chaplet is a means of reconciliation between the heart of man and the Heart of God, which is so greatly wounded by the sin of abortion."

(Blessed Mother – March 25, 2013)

"My Chaplet of the Unborn is important as it points out the error of abortion, the importance of life in the womb, and petitions a healing of heart for all who participate, in any way, in abortion. Pray it daily." *(Blessed Mother – January 29, 2014)*

HOW TO PRAY THE ROSARY OF THE UNBORN

When we pray the Rosary of the Unborn, we are asked by Heaven to:

1. Pray from the heart.
2. Call to mind Our Lady's Sorrowful Immaculate Heart.
3. Pray that hearts are convicted in the Truth about abortion.

Note: During the Rosary of the Unborn, we say the 'Glory Be' as *"All Glory be to the Father..."* and also pray *"Jesus, protect and save the unborn!"* after each Mystery, at Our Lady's request.

---

1. OPENING PRAYERS *(Optional prayers may be added.)*

(State the intention)
I/We offer this Rosary for the end to abortion and that hearts are convicted in the Truth about abortion.

(Then raise your rosary to Heaven and say:)
Celestial Queen, with this Rosary, I/we bind all sinners and all nations to Your Immaculate Heart.
(Our Lady – October 7, 1996)

The Sign of the Cross
In the Name of the Father, and of the Son, and of the Holy Spirit. Amen.

Prayer for the Conversion of Hearts
"Heavenly Father, during this time of world crisis, let all souls find their peace and security in Your Divine Will. Give each soul the grace to understand that Your Will is Holy Love in the present moment. Benevolent Father, illuminate each conscience to see the ways that he is not living in Your Will. Grant the world the grace to change and the time in which to do it. Amen." *(Mary, the Mother of God – September 28, 2001)*

Prayer to Recite with the Rosary of the Unborn
"Divine Infant Jesus, as we pray this rosary, we ask you to remove from the heart of the world the desire to commit the sin of abortion. Remove the veil of deceit Satan has placed over hearts which portrays promiscuity as a freedom, and reveal it for what it is – slavery to sin. Place over the heart of the world a renewed respect for life at the moment of conception. Amen." *(Our Lady – August 27, 2005)*

Appendix A 89

The Apostles' Creed

I believe in God, the Father Almighty, Creator of Heaven and earth; and in Jesus Christ, His only Son, Our Lord, Who was conceived by the Holy Spirit, born of the Virgin Mary, suffered under Pontius Pilate, was crucified, died, and was buried. He descended into Hell; the third day He rose again from the dead; He ascended into Heaven, and is seated at the right hand of God, the Father Almighty; from thence He shall come to judge the living and the dead. I believe in the Holy Spirit, the holy Catholic Church, the communion of saints, the forgiveness of sins, the resurrection of the body and life everlasting. Amen.

Our Father
(For the intentions of the Holy Father)

Our Father, Who art in heaven, hallowed be Thy Name. Thy Kingdom come. Thy Will be done on earth, as it is in Heaven. Give us this day our daily bread, and forgive us our trespasses, as we forgive those who trespass against us, and lead us not into temptation, but deliver us from evil. Amen.

Three (3) Hail Mary's
(Pray three Hail Mary's for an increase
of the virtues of Faith, Hope and Charity)

Hail Mary, full of grace, the Lord is with thee. Blessed art thou among women, and blessed is the fruit of thy womb, Jesus. Holy Mary, Mother of God, pray for us sinners, now and at the hour of our death. Amen.

All Glory Be

All Glory be to the Father, and to the Son, and to the Holy Spirit. As it was in the beginning, is now, and ever shall be, world without end. Amen.
(Our Lady of Guadalupe – September 21, 1995)

Fatima Prayer

O my Jesus, forgive us our sins, save us from the fires of hell, lead all souls to Heaven, especially those in most need of Thy Mercy.

Prayer for the Unborn

Jesus, protect and save the unborn!
(Mary, Refuge of Holy Love – May 19, 1998)

2. THE MYSTERIES AND PRO-LIFE INTENTIONS OF THE ROSARY

The Rosary consists of twenty (20) decades divided into four (4) sets of Mysteries (*Joyful, Luminous, Sorrowful,* and *Glorious)* depicting events in the lives of Jesus and Mary. Each set of Mysteries consists of five (5) decades, with each decade recalling a particular Mystery or event. A complete Rosary consists of praying one set of Mysteries.

When praying the Rosary of the Unborn, we use the *Pro-Life Rosary Intentions* dictated by Our Lady on June 4, 2011 *(included below)*. Meditations are optional. We recommend the *Pro-Life Meditations on the Mysteries of the Rosary* by Priests for Life:

https://www. priestsforlife.org/prayers/Rosary

PRAYERS TO RECITE DURING EACH DECADE

For each decade of the Rosary, we name the Mystery, say the Intention, read the Meditation (optional), and recite the following prayers:

Our Father... Ten (10) Hail Mary's... All Glory Be...

Fatima Prayer ... Prayer for the Unborn...

The Joyful Mysteries *(Monday and Saturday)*

1. FIRST JOYFUL MYSTERY
"We seek Blessed Mother's protection over the unborn."
The Annunciation

2. SECOND JOYFUL MYSTERY
"We pray for guidance for all involved in the abortion industry and mothers considering abortion."
The Visitation

3. THIRD JOYFUL MYSTERY
"We pray for the conversion of anyone who supports abortion."
The Nativity

4. FOURTH JOYFUL MYSTERY
"We pray for government leaders who support abortion."
The Presentation

5. FIFTH JOYFUL MYSTERY
"We pray for any religious leader who does not speak out against abortion."
The Finding of the Child Jesus in the Temple

Appendix A 91

The Luminous Mysteries *(Thursday)*

1. FIRST LUMINOUS MYSTERY
"We seek Blessed Mother's protection over the unborn."
The Baptism of Jesus in the Jordan

2. SECOND LUMINOUS MYSTERY
"We pray for guidance for all involved in the abortion industry and mothers considering abortion."
The Wedding at Cana

3. THIRD LUMINOUS MYSTERY
"We pray for the conversion of anyone who supports abortion."
Christ Proclaims the Kingdom of God

4. FOURTH LUMINOUS MYSTERY
"We pray for government leaders who support abortion."
The Transfiguration

5. FIFTH LUMINOUS MYSTERY
"We pray for any religious leader who does not speak out against abortion."
The Institution of the Eucharist

The Sorrowful Mysteries *(Tuesday and Friday)*

1. FIRST SORROWFUL MYSTERY
"We seek Blessed Mother's protection over the unborn."
The Agony in the Garden

2. SECOND SORROWFUL MYSTERY
"We pray for guidance for all involved in the abortion industry and mothers considering abortion."
The Scourging at the Pillar

3. THIRD SORROWFUL MYSTERY
"We pray for the conversion of anyone who supports abortion."
The Crowning with Thorns

4. FOURTH SORROWFUL MYSTERY
"We pray for government leaders who support abortion."
The Carrying of the Cross

5. FIFTH SORROWFUL MYSTERY
"We pray for any religious leader who does not speak out against abortion."
The Crucifixion and Death of Our Lord

The Glorious Mysteries *(Wednesday and Sunday)*

---

1. FIRST GLORIOUS MYSTERY
"We seek Blessed Mother's protection over the unborn."
The Resurrection

2. SECOND GLORIOUS MYSTERY
"We pray for guidance for all involved in the abortion industry and mothers considering abortion."
The Ascension

3. THIRD GLORIOUS MYSTERY
"We pray for the conversion of anyone who supports abortion."
The Descent of the Holy Spirit

4. FOURTH GLORIOUS MYSTERY
"We pray for government leaders who support abortion."
The Assumption

5. FIFTH GLORIOUS MYSTERY
"We pray for any religious leader who does not speak out against abortion."
The Coronation of Mary as Queen of Heaven and Earth

3. <u>**CLOSING PRAYERS**</u> *(Optional prayers may be added.)*

Hail, Holy Queen, Mother of Mercy! Our life, our sweetness and our hope! To Thee do we cry, poor banished children of Eve; to Thee do we send up our sighs, mourning and weeping in this valley of tears. Turn, then, most Gracious Advocate, Thine Eyes of mercy toward us, and after

Appendix A 93

this our exile, show unto us the blessed Fruit of Thy Womb, Jesus. O clement, O loving, O sweet Virgin Mary.

V. Pray for us, O Holy Mother of God.
R. That we may be made worthy of the promises of Christ.

Let us pray. O God, Whose Only Begotten Son, by His life, death and resurrection, has purchased for us the rewards of eternal life, grant, we beseech Thee, that meditating upon these Mysteries of the most Holy Rosary of the Blessed Virgin Mary, we may imitate what they contain, and obtain what they promise through the same Christ, Our Lord. Amen.

(For the intentions and well-being of the Holy Father)
Our Father...   Hail Mary...   All Glory Be...

The Sign of the Cross
In the Name of the Father, and of the Son,
and of the Holy Spirit. Amen.

October 8, 2021
Pray the Rosary of the Unborn

The Blessed Virgin Mary says: "Praise be to Jesus."

"Dear children, once again, I ask you to be faithful to the recitation of the rosary. Pray the Rosary of the Unborn with faith that this most heinous of sins – abortion – will be recognized for what it is. The longer you slaughter your unborn, the farther your nation and the world drift away from Papa God. The abyss between Heaven and earth is already wider than even in the days of Noah or Sodom and Gomorrah."

"The Rosary of the Unborn has the potential to stop this crime and to mitigate the damage that has been done between Heaven and earth. Your prayers on this rosary are healing."

Read Jonah 3:1-10

APPENDIX B

FAMILY CONSECRATION TO THE UNITED HEARTS

INSTRUCTIONS

1. Gather your family.
2. Read the Message from St. Thomas Aquinas and the two Scripture passages.
3. Recite the prayers given. *(Daily recitation is recommended.)*
4. Display the *Complete Image of the United Hearts* and the Image of *Mary, Refuge of Holy Love*, in your home.

St. Thomas Aquinas comes. He bows and prays before the tabernacle. He says: *"Praise be to Jesus."* He sits ... *"You know the times are perilous. There is much speculation about the future. People live in fear, not trust. It is time for families to be consecrated to the United Hearts and to make a personal consecration to The Flame of Holy Love. This will be like the lamb's blood on the portal of their hearts and homes. Evil will pass over them and by them." (October 31, 2001)*

2 Chronicles – Chapter 7, vs. 16

For now I have chosen and consecrated this house so that My Name may be there forever; My Eyes and My Heart will be there for all time.

Exodus – Chapter 12, vs. 7 and vs.13

Then they shall take some of the blood and put it on the two doorposts and the lintel of the houses in which they eat them. The blood shall be a sign for you, upon the houses where you are; and when I see the blood, I will pass over you, and no plague shall fall upon you to destroy you when I smite the land of Egypt.

Consecration to the Flame of Holy Love

Immaculate Heart of Mary, humbly, I ask that You take my heart into the Flame of Holy Love, that is the Spiritual Refuge of all mankind. Do not look upon my faults and failings, but allow these iniquities to be burned away by this purifying Flame. Through Holy Love, help me to be sanctified in the present moment, and in so doing, give to You, dear Mother, my every thought, word, and action. Take me and use me according to Your

Appendix B   95

great pleasure. Allow me to be Your instrument in the world, all for the greater glory of God and towards Your victorious reign. Amen.

Dedication of Homes to Mary, Refuge of Holy Love

Mary, my Mother, my Fortress – Refuge of Holy Love – sanctify this home through Holy Love. Open each heart that dwells herein to holiness. Lead us along the path of Holy Love. Be victorious over any evil, whether it be an unknown force within these walls, a seductive habit, or some voluntary attachment we have chosen ourselves. Make this home a sanctuary of Holy Love. Amen.

Consecration of Families to the United Hearts of Jesus and Mary

Sacred and United Hearts of Jesus and Mary, You are one in purpose as You desire the salvation, holiness, and sanctity of each soul. We consecrate our family to You seeking Your victory both in our hearts and in the world. We acknowledge the perfection of Your mercy in the past, the abundance of Your provision in the future, and the supreme sovereignty of the Father's Divine Will in this present moment. We desire to be part of Your triumphant reign beginning in this present moment through our 'yes' to Holy and Divine Love. We wish, with the help of Your Grace, to live out this consecration through every future moment. Thus we will be united in triumph with You, dear United Hearts of Jesus and Mary. Amen.

Marriage Consecration *(Optional)*

Holy and Sacred United Hearts of Jesus and Mary, we consecrate our marriage to You today in this present moment. Through this consecration, we will dedicate our hearts to Your victory. United in You we seek Your protection and provision. Increase our love for You and for each other with every breath we take. Regally clothe our hearts in the Divine Will of the Eternal Father. Help us to increase in holiness in and through Your United Hearts. Amen.

Children's Consecration to the United Hearts *(Optional)*

Dear United Hearts of Jesus and Mary, I love You very much. I want to give You this present moment and all the future moments of my life. I always want to please You. I give You my heart today and always, and pray You will unite it to Your United Hearts. Place in my heart, dear Jesus and Mary, the desire to help sinners turn to You. Amen.

APPENDIX C

CONCERNING PHOTOGRAPHS

"My daughter, I am prepared to share with you some knowledge of the images that have been captured on photographs. Keep in mind, however, that this is what photographs are – images captured on film. Different images have different meaning to each individual. Therefore, each picture should be surrendered to prayer before conclusions are drawn. First, let Me begin with the cloud seen hovering over the Prayer Center on certain nights of prayer. This is a sign of God's Presence and protection over you. The Jews in the desert had such an escort. The color purple stands for Jesus' Passion. Red is for martyrdom. Green is for hope. The circle is My signature – whether large or seen as a small Host shape. St. Pio is your special patron on the property and in this Mission, thus his presence in some pictures. It is My intent that these simple explanations will help My children. But if they pray, they will know in their hearts the full meaning of each image. Further, their pilgrimage should not be a search for signs but a search for perfection in holiness." *(Our Lady – November 8, 1996)*

"I invite all to pilgrimage to My property. Here the grace of My Heart is pouring into the world. Certain ones will be made to see Me there. Others have already captured Me in the eyes of their camera. My Statue of Sorrows comes to life as a sign of My Presence there. The flesh takes on the hue of real flesh, both to the naked eye and on film. Rosaries turn gold as a sign to all that prayer does change things. The scent of roses is further proof of My Presence. Certain saints and angels will be photographed on the property as a sign of Heaven's favor." *(Our Lady of Guadalupe – November 12, 1997)*

"Many of My angels have been caught on camera – more will be – do not be surprised." *(Mary of the Holy Angels – August 2, 2009)*

"I open My Heart here to you as never before. You will witness signs of My Grace in the form of hearts in nature and on photographs all around the property soon. This is a sign of Heaven's approval of your efforts here." *(Mary, Refuge of Holy Love – June 24, 2017)*